Return to the Source
Volume 1

Talks by
Sri Mahaprabu
A Living Enlightened Master

Collected by
Satchitanandam
Disciple of Sri Mahaprabu

Published by
Sri Satguru Annamalai Swamigal Spiritual Trust

Copyright

Published by
Sri Satguru Annamalai Swamigal Spiritual Trust
Survey number 179/2B, Paliapattu, Chengam Taluk
Tiruvannamalai District, Tamil Nadu 606704
annamalaiswamytrust@gmail.com
www.SriAnnamalaiSwami.org
Phone: 9150741455, 9994595425, 9159888842

Bhagavan Ramana Maharshi

Sri Mahaprabu

Table of Contents

Note from the Recorder

This book has the power to transform your life. Not just by its content, but by your coming in touch with the Master from whose lips these words of Wisdom have been spoken. Sri Mahaprabu is an enlightened Master from Tiruvannamalai, India who has been quietly guiding a small group of sincere seekers for over 17 years.

Before meeting Sri Mahaprabu in 2019, I was searching to fill a deep void that was eating into an otherwise very successful position in life. I was the founder & CEO for a US based technology company for over 15 years and was serving the community at various levels. Still, this feeling of incompleteness, combined with a deep thirst to fill it, continued to possess me. I spent a few years immersing myself in Vedantic study along with reading the works of great Masters from across the world. And yet I found that despite all the book knowledge, deep down I was completely in the dark as to who I really am. Making matters worse, I could sense how all this accumulated knowledge was only strengthening my ego. This took the suffering to another level.

It was sheer grace and a miraculous set of circumstances that found me at the feet of Sri Mahaprabu one evening at his house. That day my life changed forever. I began to see firsthand how an Enlightened One lives in this world. An embodiment of Love and Intelligence, flowing moment to moment in harmony, in total Surrender, with things happening around him in perfection. While his message was exactly that of all the great Sages, the way he communicated it so I could understand its deep import, and the divine presence from which those words were uttered, began to resonate with me deeply. After innumerable Satsang sessions with him, my doubts, misconceptions and misunderstandings began to evaporate. And in their place blossomed a clarity I had never had before. It took a long time to come out of the effects of the knowledge overload I had accumulated. Then, after sitting for long sessions with him, listening to his deep insights, followed by hours of silence in his presence, I began to get in touch with a never-before-experienced feeling which was both within me and without. Something of an indescribable quality that shined in bright contrast to the turmoil and ugliness that has been tormenting me inside for years.

By grace, the thought occurred to me early on to record our conversations with his permission. I did it for my own help. Those precious words should not fall through the cracks of my memory. I would listen to them again and again. Later came the thought that I should share this invaluable treasure with other seekers like me. I approached Sri Mahaprabu who readily agreed and in his characteristic way said "Let it happen. IT will decide when." Almost two years later, for the first time now, his talks are being made aware to the world in the form of this book. The first in a series we hope to bring out.

These talks cover all the essential topics including: Our Fundamental Problem, Why we suffer, All about the Mind, Body and Soul, How to deal with Worry, Fear, Anger, Desire, How to transcend the ego, Realize our True Self, and Experience Eternal Freedom.

The best part about all these talks is that they do not require any special knowledge or background on the part of the reader to understand and imbibe the message, since they simply beautifully kindle the presence of THAT which is already within each of us. Sri Mahaprabu is a Master at bringing it out and putting us in touch with the Truth.

How to use this book

Please read the introduction to Sri Mahaprabu and his Journey, followed by the first couple of talks. After that, there is no prescribed order to follow. Please go to whatever topic that could be of help to you at that moment.

It is my sincere prayer that you find this book as a stepping stone to the real solution that ends all your suffering - Coming under the auspices of a living enlightened Master like Sri Mahaprabu.

Sincerely

Satchitanandam
Disciple of Sri Mahaprabu

Sri Mahaprabu

Introduction

Sri Mahaprabu is a *Brahma Jnāni*, who attained liberation in the year 2003 by the grace of Bhagavan Ramana Maharshi. Since 2006 he has been conducting *satsang* regularly near Tiruvannamalai. The following is a brief introduction to Sri Mahaprabu.

Venkatesan (birth name of Sri Mahaprabu) was born into a very ordinary family in southern Tamil Nadu. It wasn't until he was in his teen years that a very strong desire began to consume the youth. The desire to know about birth, death and who he really was. Seeing death all around him at a young age and realizing the certainty of his own death strengthened this desire into an unstoppable urge, one that must have been simmering and evolving for many lives past. This single-pointedness brought him to Tiruvannamalai in the year 1993.

Entering Ramanasramam for the first time, he saw the board which described Sri Bhagavan's death experience in detail. He instantly knew he had come to the right place where all his questions would be answered. Being a sincere devotee of Lord Annamalaiyar (Shiva) and Sri Bhagavan Ramana Maharshi, it was by sheer grace that he was soon connected with Sri Annamalai Swami Ashram in Pelakottu (adjacent to Sri Ramanasramam). He would go there regularly to attend the various *parayanas* being conducted, as well as for the monthly Swathi Puja of Sri Annamalai Swami.

He used to spend most of his time in meditation at the forests of Arunachala hill, Bhagavan Sri Ramana's *samādhi* and Sri Annamalai Swami's *samādhi* shrine. He diligently pursued the path of self-enquiry taught by Sri Bhagavan and Sri Annamalai Swami. Thus, for 10 years he underwent a rigorous *sādhana*, unwavering in his determination despite numerous trials and tribulations, thanks to his burning desire to know the Truth, his steadfast *bhakti* (devotion) and his strong faith in Bhagavan. And on January 1st, 2003 'IT' happened. The dissolution of the individual into the universal. Sri Mahaprabu was born.

For the next forty days, he was mostly in a state of blissful *samādhi* going into indescribable depths of experience. The next three years were spent mostly in solitude, revelling in a state that words cannot describe. Not only did his spiritual friends observe a significant change in his lifestyle but were able to feel a tremendous silence in his presence. They began to share their questions with him and received an inner clarity they had never experienced before.

In 2006, Sri Mahaprabu received a divine message from Lord Buddha who instructed him to share his experiences and guide true seekers of the Truth. With the blessings of Sri Buddha, Mahaprabu started his *satsangs* in Paliappattu (a small village at the outskirts of Tiruvannamalai) in 2006. Devotees of Annamalai Swami including Sri Sundaram Swami who was the caretaker and disciple of Annamalai Swami for 21 years, began to attend these *satsangs*. Sri Annamalai Swami, before his *Maha-samādhi* in 1995, had told Sundaram Swami that another living enlightened master will come to guide him towards enlightenment. Sundaram Swami and other trustees were able to recognise Sri Mahaprabu, as the living enlightened master that Sri Annamalai Swami had predicted and have been continuing their spiritual *sādhana* under the guidance of Sri Mahaprabu till date.

Various seekers of the Truth from different parts of Tamil Nadu and abroad started attending *satsang* with Sri Mahaprabu. Among them, Sri Mahaprabu began to guide only those seekers who are sincere, dedicated and truly committed to realising the Truth in this very birth. His *satsangs* and meditation camps are happening regularly in Paliapattu, Tiruvannamalai.

Satsang

Being in *satsang* with Sri Mahaprabu is like simultaneously diving to the deepest depths of *jnāna* and soaring to the highest peaks of *bhakti*, shepherded throughout by a sweet and fragrant power that is none other than Love.

Since it is the Supreme Power that speaks and acts through that bodily frame, **there are no traditional rules, methods, techniques, not even scheduled timings. Yet *satsang* happens as sure as day follows night and night, day.**

During *satsang*, hours can pass by like minutes, as we join him in meditation, or melting to his devotional singing, or listening to the words of great *jnānis* (Bhagavan Ramana Maharshi, Annamalai Swami, Ramakrishna Paramahamsa, Adi Sankaracharya, Buddha, Osho, Sadhu Om, Avudaya Akkal, Vallalar Swamigal, Bharathiyar and Thayumanavar to name a few) or just sitting spellbound by the words of wisdom that flow so beautifully and spontaneously from Sri Mahaprabu's lips. Words that shatter all preconceived notions, **resulting in a clarity that no book or teacher can ever come close to giving.** Only a *Brahma jñāni* like Mahaprabu can.

No question goes unanswered. And yet he reminds us that it is the questioner that needs to disappear. "Meditation is always happening," he says. "It is the one who wants to meditate, that needs to dissolve. **The Experience being sought is already there and is not something to be attained. It happens only when 'you' are not there to experience it.**" *Satsang* with Mahaprabu is undoubtedly the greatest, best-kept secret, not just in Tiruvannamalai but in this entire world.

Perfection

Just being in Sri Mahaprabu's presence and observing how he carries himself, gives you a glimpse into what perfection is. **Every movement, every gesture, every word comes from a point of total calm, total presence, without the slightest agitation whatsoever; whether he is in the market or in *satsang*.**

Next to him, our actions stand in stark contrast; hurried on the outside, spurred by the turbulence inside. And he knows it. Nothing escapes his watchfulness, even though he is not looking at you. "With Awareness, With Awareness" are the words you will hear him say so often.

Unique approach

A look back at history reveals how the Supreme Power manifests itself as *Brahma jñānis* in different eras; each of them so different in their post-enlightenment life as it were. Some stay silent, some serve as a beacon to those who come, while others become a light that spreads far and wide.

Sri Mahaprabu's uniqueness is this: Once he embraces a sincere seeker, **he comes down to his or her level, working tirelessly with the seeker, day after day, at every step in the journey.** And he even says as much, that "ensuring the disciple attains *jñāna* in this very life, is all that I work for." Such is the boundless love and compassion that he IS.

Sri Mahaprabu continuously **creates situations for the disciple** to serve and to be in *satsang* with him. It is this combination of *satsang* and *seva*, classroom-learning and real-world practice, in close contact with the Guru that weakens the grip of the ego over time. And after continuous, repeated erosion, it finally surrenders. "Only when you have totally surrendered, can the Truth even enter", says Mahaprabu.

Bhagavan Ramana Maharshi once said, "A disciple in the hands of a Guru, is like prey caught in the mouth of a tiger. There is no escape possible." **That Tiger is Sri Mahaprabu.**

Sri Mahaprabu's Journey

Sri Mahaprabu attributes his enlightenment entirely to Sri Bhagavan Ramana Maharshi. **"Adhu Bhagavan potta pichai" (that is the alms that Bhagavan gave this beggar)** he often says.

This picture of Bhagavan is framed in Sri Sadhu Om Hall, where Sri Mahaprabu conducts Satsang.

THIS IS THE JOURNEY OF A YOUNG BOY FROM A SMALL VILLAGE IN TAMIL NADU WHO WOULD BECOME CONSUMED BY THE QUESTION 'WHO AM I' AND PURSUED IT TILL THE END, RESULTING IN HIS AWAKENING.

THE CONTENT BELOW IS RECORDED ENTIRELY FROM SATSANGS WITH MAHAPRABU DURING THOSE OCCASIONS WHEN HE WOULD RECOLLECT THE PAST. THESE ARE HIS WORDS, ADDRESSED BY HIM IN 3rd or 1st PERSON.

Childhood

Venkatesan (birth name of Sri Mahaprabu) was born on 11th July, 1974 in Namakkal, Tamil Nadu (his maternal home) and grew up in Pudhuamma Palayam, Perambalur District, near Trichy. He came from a typical conservative, middle-class family. His schooling from 2nd grade through 12th, was in nearby Thurayoor. He was the eldest child, with a sister and brother.

When Mahaprabu recalls his childhood, the one thing that stands out was his loving nature, a loving heart for all things and beings, especially human beings. His love was such that he would touch a leaf and embrace it, pray to any mountain he saw and shed tears at the sight of any suffering. He was especially loving to his parents, who were no less than God for him. At nights out of sheer love and gratitude, he would massage his mother's feet till she asked him to stop. His father kept a distance and wouldn't encourage it, so the boy would wait till his father slept and then massage his feet. He was especially close to his grandfather, who was a very quiet and hard-working man who largely kept to himself. He too was very fond of the boy. Sri Mahaprabu remembers a song that his grandfather used to sing to him often. *Ulagalam unarndhu vodhuvadharku ariyavam...* Years later, when Sri Mahaprabu entered the big temple at Tiruvannamalai for the very first time, imagine his surprise when he saw this song inscribed on the temple walls. He took it as a very good sign.

From young, he was inclined to only speak the Truth, even if he knew it would cause harm in certain situations. He was also highly energetic and cheerful, always on the move and was never one to waste any time. His loving nature combined with this high energy propelled him to help others a lot. He would help as much as he could at home and outside. In school he always excelled in academics, thanks to a sharp focus he had which kept him very attentive in class. At home he would daily recollect and assimilate what was taught. This was enough. He did not have to study much for exams and yet would top his class. This continued all the way to high school where he earned several accolades in education and extra-curricular activities.

The Jolt of Death

When he was 12 years old, his dear grandfather died. Seeing death for the first time, especially the death of one who was so dear to him had a deep impact on the child. He saw the anguish of those around the body, how it was taken from the house and cremated. So many questions began to torment him: Can he hear us crying? Where will he go now? He went to the burial ground and was the last one to leave. While there, he was almost mad and at the same time was observing things with the objective mind of a scientist. Won't this happen to me? It is going to happen for sure. This was the first time he sensed these kinds of questions in him about life. **This event was the main reason why he turned to Jnāna.**

He also had an inner fear of death. He feared for the death of his parents, his brother and sister, his own death. As fate would have it, he would soon witness so much death around him. His grandmother committed suicide a few years later. A close friend and classmate of his died in an accident. The entire body was burnt. Mahaprabu himself took the body to the hospital for the post-mortem and then to the burial ground and cremated him. His *virakthi* (frustration) was at its peak. When is my time to die? I was speechless for 3 days. All your education, skill, money will all go to mud. Born as a fool, you will die as a fool. This kept pricking me so painfully. Soon another close friend of his would die by drowning in a lake nearby. Mahaprabu remembers the incident clearly. He saw a crowd at the lake and asked what happened. He remembers immediately taking off his shirt and diving into the deep waters to save him. But alas, he could only retrieve the dead body. All this had a tremendous impact on the young mind. The questions about life and death became stronger and more compelling.

Pharmacy College - A turning point

After completing his schooling with honours (he not only topped his class but also was one of the toppers in the entire district), in 1991 he joined a two-year program at a college of Pharmacy, where he began to learn about the human body and medicine. A point to be noted here is that Mahaprabu had no interest in pharmacy or the life-sciences. His academic interests were in Engineering and his top scores would have easily gotten him admission to any college of his choice. Yet his father intervened and insisted that he become a doctor. Mahaprabu tried protesting, telling him that he was not interested, nor did he have the required scores in those subjects to get admission into medical college. His father wouldn't budge. To not displease him further, the young lad gave in. As he did not get admission into medical college, he had to settle for a 2-year course in Pharmacy. Why this is so relevant is that at the time of his graduation from high school, there was no engineering college in Tiruvannamalai. Only after 2 years would it be built and commence. How beautifully nature has guided the boy, making him wait

2 years, just so he could come to study in Tiruvannamalai, the *Jnana Bhoomi* – Land of Enlightenment.

An important phase of his pharmacy education was the training program before graduation. He was assigned to the post-mortem unit of a big hospital. The 90 days that followed, would change him forever. Day in and day out he witnessed so much death. Bodies would come and pile up. Many were accident or suicide victims. He was asked to do post-mortems on them. Slicing open bodies, hands drenched in blood, he would remove organs such as the intestines, heart, brain and examine them. This happened on a daily basis. Soon he lost all sense of normalcy. Daily he would wake up, go to work sitting in the bus like one who is possessed, put in long hours working in such a horrifying environment and return home, only to go back the next day. He was like a zombie.

On the one hand he saw the world racing forward with people entertaining hope and enjoyment, while death kept coming unannounced and unmercifully through accidents, crimes and natural causes. **He was shaken to the core of his being**.

After graduating, he spent a few months working in various nearby villages that did not have access to doctors or medical help. He soon realized the inability of modern medicines to cure diseases. Added to that, he saw their harmful side effects. This created a serious conflict in him. One of ethics. He could not accept such a profession for the rest of his life. So he made a strong decision to change career paths. With great difficulty, he convinced his father that he would pursue an Engineering degree.

Coming to Tiruvannamalai

One evening as he was laying on his bed in a state of total despair, not knowing who he was and no one to help, he had this vision. It was over-powering. He saw in a flash, several births of his. Where he was living with different parents and different siblings in each birth. It happened so fast, yet so clearly was it seen. He was shocked beyond belief. He realized that this is how each birth was being passed. Totally believing that he was an individual as told by his parents, that he had a family, he lived with them, for them, but only to die and take on a totally different body and different parents without any regard whatsoever for his previous father and mother. At that moment he lost all his attachment towards his parents, siblings, possessions and life itself. He decided to leave. He could not stay with them a day longer. Remember, this was the boy who would die for his parents.

The very next day he received a telegram from the engineering college in Tiruvannamalai confirming his admission. He saw this as a glimmer of hope and thanked the Supreme Power.

As mentioned earlier, fate would ensure that Tiruvannamalai saw its first engineering college open that very year as though it was built just for Mahaprabu to come to Tiruvannamalai. He got admission there and soon found himself on a bus heading to a place known for its great jnanis (jnana bhoomi) but without the slightest notion about it, or about Jnana. Yet there was this unmistakable deep thirst in him to know who he really was.

For the next 10 years, he would be consumed with finding the answers to those questions that reverberated in him stronger and stronger. Who Am I. Where did I come from? How did I enter this mother's womb? When I die what will happen? Will I enter another womb? Then what is the purpose of this life attached to these parents, if I am going to repeat it all over again with another family? My entire foundation was destroyed. How many lives I would have lived and died and married and died, different relations, so many fears, jealousies, anger, revenges. And yet I could feel a love deep inside me. I wondered why it doesn't come out. I decided that whatever happens, I will find out who I am.

Engineering College

The 4 years from 1993-1997 was simply a way to get away from home and be in solitude while searching for the answers to life's questions that consumed me. Even though I was a student who topped his class and had aspirations for a successful career when young, now things had changed entirely. I had no interest whatsoever in a commercial path. I used to think: All that I need is a small room to stay, 2 times a day food for this small stomach, 2 shirts, 2 dhotis and 2 towels. Imagine, this was my attitude at the age of 19!

As soon as I reached Tiruvannamalai I heard about a jnani named Yogi Ram Surat Kumar. I remember people saying that meeting a Jnani was a good thing for seekers. I had *darshan* of him. Then I saw the entrance to Ramanashramam. I went in. There was a board there that described the death experience that Bhagavan had as a young boy, and how he left home to come to Tiruvannamalai. That gave me hope that I had finally come to the right place too, Tiruvannamalai. I prayed to Bhagavan sincerely, but beyond that there was no connection.

As I started my studies, the inner frustration continued. I felt the entire world was empty and life was meaningless. All are going to die but they are ignoring that totally with not even a mosquito bite of a sensation, they are all living as though they are permanent. Totally dejected and desperate, I decided to go to the famous Siva Temple in Tiruvannamalai. I remember going in through the North entrance. This was the first time I was entering the temple. There I saw many verses were inscribed on the walls. But there was this verse right in front of me. I read it:

Jnana tabodanarai va endru azaikum malai Annamalai.
Annamalai is the mountain that welcomes seekers of Jnana.

Suddenly, all the energy that I had lost in 3 years, flowed through the body in a rush. It felt like it was 1 Lakh watts of electricity. Though the mind created this feeling, it was a huge tonic for me. A huge boost. I decided to focus on this exclusively from now on.

But in my 2nd year, I faced setbacks in the form of health. An accident in the gym hurt affected my right hand for a long time. That same year I developed an illness that made me bed-ridden for 15 days. I couldn't even get up. It was as though I was paralyzed. A fever would come and go. As a result of all this, my studies began to take a hit. And then tragedy struck again the next year. Another close friend was involved in an accident. I rushed him to Chennai and admitted him in a hospital. Fortunately, the boy would survive. I returned the very next day to Tiruvannamalai to write my final exam. I remember sitting in the examination hall, shirt full of blood stains. I failed that exam. More failures would follow. The arrears (failed subjects) piled up. There were 14 of them I had to clear. Despite all the frustrations I knew that I had to successfully complete the degree. It was a matter of survival. I began to study hard and take up the arrear exams in addition to my current semester exams. I remember sitting in those examination halls like a dead body. Only the hand would move while writing the exam. There was no enthusiasm at all. I felt like I was possessed. Total frustration. I was doing it just to complete the cycle. A dead body taking up the pen to write something. That was how it happened. And yet I passed all his exams, unbelievably clearing all 14 arrears alongside. I could now graduate.

Finding a Job

As graduation neared, Mahaprabu wondered what he was going to do. I had almost become mad. One thing is for sure. One day this body will go. Before that I need to find out Who I am. **I will not leave Tiruvannamalai till I find out. Even if this body dies it is OK.** I just wanted minimum money for one meal a day and a place to stay in Tiruvannamalai. Friends in college were applying for jobs in big cities and abroad. Many of them left. I had no interest in all that. I approached the owner of the hotel where I would eat daily. I begged him for a job in the hotel where food and boarding would be provided with a minimal salary. He was shocked that I was serious but didn't think it was appropriate for me to take up such a job given my education. As a last resort I was even to live on the street and beg for food so I could stay in Tiruvannamalai and continue my practice.

I finally turned to Lord Siva (Annamalai Temple) with extreme devotion. I sat there crying and begged. "Please do not make me leave Tiruvannamalai without knowing who I am. Keep me here even as a beggar, but please don't send me away." At that time a friend of mine happened to come to the temple. Seeing the tears on my face, he said 'Come with me. I will take you to someone who can help you.' I was then introduced to Thiruvadithuli Swami. A great *bhakta* (devotee of Lord Panduranga). Even though he did not conduct *satsang* or answer Mahaprabu's deep questions, I found a joy in serving him. For nearly 5 years I served Thiruvadithuli Swami continuously. I remember helping wherever possible. Be it in the kitchen or cleaning all the toilets regularly, especially on crowded days.

Miraculously (just like how an engineering college was opened in Tiruvannamalai the very year that Mahaprabu was looking for admission) a private polytechnic college was inaugurated in Tiruvannamalai, and he was offered a job as a lecturer there. Now he was assured that he could stay in Tiruvannamalai and pursue his *sadhana*. Nothing else was more important. His gratitude towards the Supreme Power became stronger and stronger.

And from that year 1997 onwards, something began to pull him inside to just sit. **He did not know it was meditation back then, but it kept pulling him to sit.** So many times, whenever there was a chance, he would sit quietly. After graduation when everyone left the hostel, he stayed alone in that big building (he was the hostel warden too) for 45 days. Most of that time was spent sitting silently. Soon he was at a stage where he could not avoid sitting.

His *seva* to Thiruvadithuli Swami continued till 2002. In those 5 years, he would visit Ramanashramam mainly because Thiruvadithuli Swami conducted *satsang* in the nearby Annamalai Swami Ashram.

Marriage

For someone who was so single-pointed about knowing the Truth, and who lived his life like a total renunciate, it is surprising that the thought of marriage would enter his life. This is how Mahaprabu recalls it happening.

During the engineering college years from 1993-1997, while coming by bus from his town to Tiruvannamalai, he would usually sleep. But each and every time, he would automatically wake up at a particular place called Ulundurpet, when the bus passed by the temple built for Sri Ramakrishna Paramahamsa. He felt a strong connection to Sri Paramahamsa. He decided to visit the temple. It was January 1st. He went in and sat in the hall with other devotees but in total silence inside. A Swami was coming by, blessing each devotee by touching their head. Just as his turn was coming, Mahaprabu remembers a single thought that consumed him: I want to attain *Jnana* in this very birth itself. At that moment the Swami blessed him. Mahaprabu later found out that it was the celebrated 'Kalpataru Day' in remembrance of the day when Sri Paramahamsa blessed everyone under the Kalpataru tree at the Cosipore garden house.

Mahaprabu continued: It then happened that year when I was sitting in meditation for a long time, Sri Ramakrishna Paramahamsa appeared to Mahaprabu and told the following: "You will get married. Children will be born. If you go against it, it will still happen. You cannot stop it, so don't fight it. Don't worry about it. But it will not be an obstacle for you. Just live like a *bhakta*."

At that time Mahaprabu had the least interest in women, marriage or even the idea of marriage. But he respected the words of this great saint and let things happen. And it happened exactly as predicted, in the year 2000.

Sadhana

I had made it very clear to my family that *sadhana* was my main priority in life. Other than my wife and son I had dropped all other family connections a long time ago. Even my parents. My love for them was still the same. I would call them once every 3 months and enquire. But no visits, no matter what the occasion. There was tremendous pressure from all sides. 'Why are you not coming to the wedding? Why aren't you doing this for us? Why are you always sitting in *dhyanam*?' So much opposition I had to deal with, at home and from outside. But as my understanding was very clear, my decision was firm. I knew these were all not real. **But I still did not know who I was. That was unbearable. I had to find out.** The determination was very strong.

Once I felt the peace inside, I was always naturally drawn towards sitting and going deep within. I stayed away from books and external guides. People would often say 'This book is great; you should read it. You can take it.' My reply was 'Please, if you want to see me again, don't raise this topic again.

What I need is already inside here. I know it is not out there. I have gone inside. You also please go inside.'

Every day I would wake up at 4 AM and sit in *dhyanam*. At 5:30 I would pick up a friend on my moped and go to the forest. He would sit at a certain spot. I would go further inside and sit. We would be there till 8 AM. Then I would come home and get ready to leave for work. At the college, I told all the staff that I will only speak during class hours. That I was paid to do that. Outside class if anyone wanted to speak to me, I would kindly request them to please write it on a paper and I will reply in writing. I would urge them to please help me in my practice by agreeing to this. In the college, I would meditate whenever I had time. To avoid being seen, I would go to the library and sit behind the end of the shelves. In the lab, I would sit behind heavy machinery. On returning home, I would wash and almost immediately leave to that same spot in the forest, sit there for over an hour and return around 7 pm. Then I would take the wife and son to Ramanashramam. On the way I would get them some snacks. They would sit at the entrance. I would sit in Bhagavan's *Samadhi*. This was a daily routine.

Bhagavan Ramana

To me Bhagavan was everything. He was my father. It was exactly like a son living with his father and coming to see him in his room. I saw the room where I lived and the ashram as part of the same house in Tiruvannamalai. I would speak to Bhagavan from the heart. 'How are you father? I am doing well.' It was a very deep and affectionate connection. I would sit there till 9:30 PM till they asked me to leave.

I would then ask the family if they wanted to eat something and get them what they wanted. Straight we would head to the Girivalam path where it splits from the main road. Wife and son would sit near some trees, a bit away from me. I would sit there in total stillness. Till 11 pm I will be there. They would never call me or disturb me. This was my daily routine.

On Sundays, as there was no college, I would make the most of it. After getting whatever was needed for the home, I would leave for Virupaksha cave around 9:30 AM. I would pack some date fruits and water. This was my lunch. Sitting in the cave I would tell myself strongly: O Mind. You have everything you need for the rest of the day. No work is there for you. Snacks are also here. The only allowance for the body is to go to the toilet. With this determination I would sit in Virupaksha cave for hours together. Around lunch time I would eat the dates, drink the water and again sit. Only in the evening around 5:30 or 6 PM,

I would get up. The whole body used to tremble with hunger. I would come down the steps and go to a tea shop, have a tea to get some energy and go home. This was the routine every Sunday.

2002 - The Crucial Year

The year 2002 was when Venkatesan had no choice but to leave Thiruvadithuli Swami. He had dedicated 5 years to serving him but found himself no closer to finding the Truth about himself. And no help was coming from the Swami. He remembers that day at the Mettur bus stand waiting for the bus to Tiruvannamalai. He knew he would never go back to Thiruvadithuli Swami. Five precious years had gone by and yet he found himself nowhere closer to the answers he was seeking. I felt totally lost and abandoned. Did not know where I was going in my spiritual *sadhana*. There was this extreme desire to know the Truth but there was no proper guidance at all. No Guru who could hold his hand and take him. Frustration was at its peak. I began to physically collapse. I almost felt like I was going to die in that bus stand. I could feel my heartbeat slowing down. It was like a heart attack coming. It was with these thoughts that I nearly collapsed. I simply laid down flat on the bench there.

It was then that the voice of Bhagavan Ramana Maharshi came to me loud and clear. "I am here for you. Why don't you try me one time?" This gave me the energy to get up and somehow reach Tiruvannamalai.

I went straight to Ramanashramam and prostrated to Bhagavan. **There the same voice came again and instructed me to read the book 'Ramana Vazhi' by Sri Sadhu Om.**

I read the book and I read it one time only. Instantly I was able to see where all I had made mistakes in the past 5 years. All my *sadhana* had been rooted in the idea of a person. I had accepted that this person existed. That was the mistake. I decided that going forward I will never give room to the idea of a person. It was Sadhu Om that gave me life again. Without him, there would be no Mahaprabu.

Mahaprabu enhanced his meditation much more. He was mostly alone or in the forest by the Girivalam road.

The point is that this much strong *Vairagya* came from the previous *janma*. Not this birth. Without even a living Guru to help him, he was able to progress. Mahaprabu did come across many teachers, but always could see that he was ahead of where they were. He had gone very deep. The only thing he was missing was the actual experience. Only the match had to be struck for the fire to catch on.

So Mahaprabu analyzed his mind deeply. He found only two issues. Fear and Worry. Fear was always about the future. Yet I cannot change the future. Worry always stemmed from the past. Yet I cannot change the past. These 2 drag me down all the time as if I were tied to two big rocks. So Mahaprabu made a very strong decision. I should not think of the past or future anymore. Only stay in the present. For 1-year Mahaprabu was only in the present moment. At that time a friend gave him a xerox copy of a book "Power of Now" by Eckhart Tolle. Mahaprabu did not read it, only saw the cover. After a year, Mahaprabu understood that with effort you can control the mind. But how long can you do this? The minute I stop the effort, Fear and Worry will return. I am still not free.

For one year it was a very strict practice. That year all illnesses stopped. No headache, fever, stomach pain, typhoid etc. People used to say there is a lot of *tejas* (brightness) in you. '

But life was not smooth even then. There were a lot of critical moments. His child died during delivery, one month premature. At 4 a.m. he got the news, and yet from 4:30 to 6 a.m. he still did his meditation. He arranged for money. Did all his paper corrections at the college by putting aside all thoughts. Finally in the evening he reached and moved his wife to a private hospital, took the baby to the burial ground at 9 p.m. Dug a hole and buried his first child. All with complete awareness. His close friend was with him throughout. He would become a disciple later.

When thoughts came, he just ignored them. Stay in the present. The mind won't go anywhere. This became a habit. The mind found joy in the present moment. While he was teaching class at college too, for the entire hour he would be in the present moment, while teaching. Something from the back penetrates and comes out through the mouth. Always fresh. A dynamic Stillness. After completing the full hour of teaching while being in the present moment, he would look out the window and see the Arunachala Hill. Tears would flow down his face.

And in the evening, no matter what, from 8 to 9 p.m. I was always in front of Bhagavan Ramana's Samadhi at Ramanashramam. Soon *Resagam* (expiration of breath) and *Kumbakam* (retention) happened one day. Then there was a flash: Breathing is not happening, but living is going on. The lungs keep a residual supply of air. Oxygen goes in slowly and carbon dioxide out slowly. At that point he felt every cell vibrating. It was tremendous. And then he sat watching the mountain without a single thought, except the consciousness of wanting to be in the present moment. Even that wish or will disappeared. There was a happening. *Brahmikka Thakkagara.* (Very powerful) A flash came and went. Back to the present moment.

The Previous Evening

On December 31st evening, (2002) Mahaprabu was sitting with two friends at the tea stall outside Ramanashramam. His friend told Mahaprabu, 'When I sit next to you my mind turns off by itself.' What? Mahaprabu asked, making sure he was aware in the present moment. This was a longtime friend, especially during all these *sadhana* years.

This friend then told the other friend about Karl Renz, an enlightened soul who was visiting Ramanashram and would conduct *satsangs* when he felt like. He was a free soul. Not many could understand him. A great artist and musician. He even mentioned that this Karl Renz did not accept Eckhart Tolle's Power of Now as a teaching. This caught Mahaprabu's attention. As his friend was talking, this Karl Renz was coming towards them! His friend told Mahaprabu, 'There he is!'. Karl looked like a very ordinary man with his shirt untucked. As if by impulse Mahaprabu rose and walked towards Karl and shook his hand. The friend introduced them. Karl said, "Come for *satsang* tomorrow, 10 to 11 AM"

At the time Mahaprabu was in complete surrender to the Supreme Power and had unshakable faith in IT, as IT has given us the earth, air and body, so IT alone is in control. He replied, 'If IT permits, I will come.' There was no hesitation, liking or disliking. His friend later said he spoke like a co-*Jnani*.

Enlightenment

The next day at 9:30 it came to Mahaprabu's awareness that Karlji (Mahaprabu always addresses him with the suffix *ji* for respect) had invited him for *satsang* at 10 AM. The place was across Ramanashramam. Downstairs was a mess (food serving place). Upstairs was an open room with just a thatched roof where the *satsang* was held. Mahaprabu had 100 Rs left of his salary. Using that, he bought flowers, fruit, biscuits and arrived there.

There was only one spot left, that too in the last row. About 20 feet away from Karlji. Mahaprabu didn't look at Karlji's face. Just sat with closed eyes without missing the present moment. (Even to get here, while leaving, starting his bike, climbing the steps, sitting, throughout he was always in the present moment. Nobody can imagine how sincere the practice was. 100% sincere.

Mahaprabu was just sitting, in full alertness of present moment. Inside there was a tremendous silence. Karlji was talking to a lady to his right. "You just simply drop your mind". These words somehow reached Mahaprabu who was not even in the line of hearing, even though there were numerous people talking. Mahaprabu recollected that as he was totally attentive in the present moment, those words reached his ears despite him being so far away.

On hearing those words "You just simply drop your mind", a laughter took place deep in the belly. Like a bubble forming deep under water, and on its way to the surface. It was developing into a powerful laugh, but it came out as a smile. Mahaprabu's thought was that this: "The whole problem is the very mind itself. He is saying 'Simply drop the mind'. How can you simply drop it! Sounds unrealistic."

Then came the words from Karl, as if he had read Mahaprabu's mind.
"Come on, ask the question!" (He probably saw the smile on my face)
Mahaprabu: "Myself?"
Karl: "Yes! You."
Mahaprabu: "You are telling 'Drop the mind.' But how to drop the mind?"
(Mahaprabu had not spoken much English in 6 years).

Karl: "First you check whether there is a mind to drop."

The match was struck

Mahaprabu checked. I am here. I can feel the body, feel the world, feel my own existence but I am unable to feel the existence of the mind. Ah! It hit him. Beyond words came an understanding, that all this time I have been worrying about something that doesn't exist. I had created an entity called the mind and then tried to control it. Because of the present moment practice for 1 full year his mind always had just one thought, that is to stay in the present moment. For one year, just one thought. As one paper cannot be called a book, one thought cannot be called a Mind. Mahaprabu skipped the present moment thought and became attention. **I searched deeply but could not find a trace of a mind. That was it. Then like something faster than light, I went inward. No mind! But I am there! Going deeper but I am still there. Before it was in flashes. Now it was continuous. I could stay with it. Joy, Bliss. I lost total awareness of surroundings, crowds etc. I merged into the universe. The thirst that started at 19, was quenched.**

Two hours passed. Opened eyes. Karlji hugged me, embraced me and said, "You are good". The friend who had come with me had left long ago. From then on for the next 40 days, daily 10 am to 12 noon, Mahaprabu would go there to Karlji's *satsang* and sit on the steps, just out of love for him and be immersed in deep *samadhi*. He did this for 40 days. For this he took off from work, using up all his casual leave (type of holiday allowed in India) in half-day chunks plus the Pongal holidays. He remembers a few statements of Karlji that had a deep impact on him: *'Nothing is lost, and Nothing is gained.' 'You cannot Not be yourself.' And 'The light of Shiva is not Shiva.'*

Those 40 days, daily after *satsang* he would go home and spend the next 4 hours again in deep *samadhi*, usually 1 to 5 pm.

Then one day while walking on the Girivalam path, his friend said let's go see Karlji as he was leaving. They met Karlji. He lifted Mahaprabu and dropped him. Mahaprabu also did the same. Karlji, an enlightened soul himself, told Mahaprabu that of hundreds of people, it feels like he came all the way to see Mahaprabu. 'I was not keen on making the trip to India this time, but felt that something was dragging me here. Now I know what it is.'

Mahaprabu would say later: We have to lose the idea that we have a mind. Because Mahaprabu was in total 'No Mind' state for 1 year, he was able to drop. The same words "Simply drop the mind" for a normal person wouldn't have worked, since he assumes the mind exists. For Mahaprabu there was no mind. Mahaprabu compared the stage just prior to this to an umbrella where the strap is removed and ready to be opened. Just the button needed to be pushed, but where the button was, wasn't known.

See the grace of Bhagavan. He decided, 'This boy is OK. It is time.' So, he sent a living *jnani* in the form of Karl Renz to come all the way to Tiruvannamalai in order to free me. See the importance of a living Master. Even though it took only a few minutes of interaction with a living Master, his presence was most important. Without his presence there, I don't know how much longer it would have taken or where I would have ended up. That is why I have tremendous gratitude for Bhagavan.

A young Sri Mahaprabu

The next 3 years

The next three years were spent mostly in solitude, revelling in a state that words cannot describe. He would tell us later: Mahaprabu would go through ever-increasing depths and heights in *samadhi*. He wanted to see the totality to the fullest extent that IT would allow him. And IT took him. Mahaprabu was saturated with bliss and perfectly content leading the quiet life, engaging in only the minimum required with the world.

But in 2006, on the day of Buddha Purnima, that changed. Sri Mahaprabu was in a deep silence when he began to feel very strongly, the presence of Lord Buddha. It was as if a powerful stream of energy from Buddha was entering him from above. He remembers it distinctly. The instruction came to carry the work forward. To help others. Mahaprabu had not known much about Buddha at all until then. Nor did he have any experience with the spiritual teaching. As if hearing him, **the message came from Lord Buddha: "You just go and sit. I will speak."** That was the message.

Satsang

The very next day, Sri Mahaprabu left for Tiruvannamalai. Having lost his individuality there was no plan on his part. IT guided him, just like IT had been doing since that morning in 2003. He reached Paliappatu, a small village 8 Km from Ramanashramam in Tiruvannamalai. Thus, with the blessings of Sri Buddha, Mahaprabu started his *satsangs* there in 2006.

A few seekers of the Truth from different parts of Tamil Nadu started attending *satsang* with Sri Mahaprabu. Among them, Sri Mahaprabu began to guide only those seekers who are sincere, dedicated and truly committed to realising the Truth in this very birth. His *satsangs* and meditation camps are still happening regularly in Paliapattu to date.

Talks

Who we are

It was around 10 PM. Mahaprabu had just started the *Satsang*. We joined him in Om chanting. A new seeker had visited the Rest house and joined the *Satsang*. There was silence for about 15 minutes. Then Sri Mahaprabu began to talk to her.

Mahaprabu: Tell me.

Seeker: (After introducing herself and her background) I don't want to take another birth. I have had enough.

Mahaprabu: Why?

Seeker: The seeker responded for some time about her suffering.

Mahaprabu: How long have you had this yearning?

Seeker: For over 10 years now.

What is freedom?

We should have the freedom to take another birth if we want, or not take it if we don't want. That is freedom. Now, this freedom has been with us, but we have lost it. Freedom is not something that anyone gives us. We are the ones who give up our freedom. Or in other words, we become subordinate to someone or something. So, this freedom has always been with us, but we have somehow lost it. Regaining our freedom is the struggle. Once we attain that freedom, what is the benefit? Like you said if you don't want another birth you can do it. Or if you want a specific type of birth you can do that too. This freedom is called *Moksha*, *Mukthi*, Liberation, etc. These are all names given to it. To this freedom of being able to take birth or not.

What is birth?

Only when we know what birth is, and what death is, only then we can go beyond it. Right? So what is born? Seeing with our eyes we can tell that the Body is born. No doubt in that? **But the question is: Are we that body?** Let's go deeper. This body of yours is a certain age and a certain size. At one point it was in the uterus. Was there a thought that 'I am in the uterus'? *No.* There might have been thoughts but no conceptualization that 'I am this', 'I am female' etc. Right? *Yes.*

Now go even further back. On the very first day you entered the womb as a microscopic entity. No head or limbs. A speck. A drop. Call it Y. That was the initial stage of this body that will at a later date be called 'Mary' (name of seeker). The day before that speck, that drop entered the womb where was this entity you call Mary? Nowhere. Mary wasn't half in the father and half in the mother. But this entity that is you, came from somewhere. Before the consummation of the male and female parents, it is possible there was something, which at a specific point took a body Y. Let's call that something as X. Before Y, there was X. It is as though X takes on Y in this life. Y grows and Y dies. X remains as is. So, all this birth and death is for whom? Y. Not X. Because X is eternal.

[Note: all diagrams were added by the recorder of these talks at a later time to help with his own understanding]

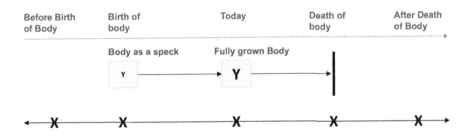

Before birth of the body Y, there was something X, which at a specific point took a body Y.

It is as though X takes on Y in this life. Y grows. Y dies. But X remains as is.

So all this birth and death is for whom? Y. Not X. Because X is eternal.

You are X.

A false assumption

Therefore should our understanding be about Y or about X? We should move our attention from the temporary Y, to that X which has been, which is, and which will be. So far no school or university has taught us how to learn about X. Only now you are entering a new phase, where you want to learn about that X. After the birth of Y, you were told by all that you were a female, a human, etc. But if all had said you were male, you would have grown up with that image. The false can always be changed. But the Truth cannot be altered. Like this, we have so many false assumptions about ourselves.

But we don't ask 'What is it that tells me I am aware of this body?' It is that X.

Our focus should be on that changeless entity X.

When you go to bed daily, you put away things like shoes, glasses, etc., and put the body on the bed. Just like you put the glasses on the table, you are putting the body on the bed. When you wake up, just like you pick up the glasses from the table, you are picking up your body from the bed. But you automatically say 'I am waking up'. You have mixed up X with Y. At that point, observe this mix-up, where you say 'I woke up'.

How can you say 'I woke up'? Did you create the body? No. So how can you take ownership of it? You don't say I am the room, I am the glasses, I am the bed. The body is also an object of your awareness, just like those other objects. Anything that is 'seen', 'observed' do you call it I? No. So, the body Y is also seen, and felt. Isn't it wrong to say I am the body? I am Y?

Feel your Existence

Close your eyes. Relax. Just listen to my words and acknowledge. If you can't say yes or no, you can simply nod your head.

Do you feel that you are existing here right now? *Yes.*

How do you know you exist? Do you have to ask yourself each time – Do I exist? *No.*

Is it your body that is telling you that you exist? *No.*

If it were merely the body, then after the death of the body also it should be aware that you exist. Something else is making you feel your existence, and because of that, you are even aware of the body.

Is it a thought that is telling you that you exist? Do you have to think in order to exist here and now? *No.*

So, the body is not telling you. Thoughts are not telling you. Yet you can feel that you exist, without any doubt.

This thing that tells you that you exist: Does it have any name? *No.* Does it have any form? *No.* Does it have any gender? *No.*

You can touch the body. Can you touch this? *No.* Can you cut it? *No.* Can you destroy it? *No.*

[There was silence for some time. A total peace prevails. Thoughts are minimal to none.]

This state of yours right now, was it there before you came here, or even a few minutes before? *No.* The tremendous suffering you mentioned, is it there now? *No.*

Did this peaceful state come from outside? Did I give it to you? *No.* So it is within you. Now, if this situation had taken place yesterday, or a month ago, wouldn't you feel the same peace? *Yes.*

So, not only is this state within, it has been with you all the while. *Yes.*

Now, go back to the time when you were in the uterus of the mother. The body (Y) was tiny. But this state would have been there also, correct? *Yes.*

This is the (X) that I am referring to. You ARE that X. Before the birth of the body Y also you are that X. Now also you are that X. After the death of the body, you are still unchanged, as X.

[Silence continued for a long time].

Now, this feeling of Existence, X, do you think it is different for each body in this room? *No.*

So then, X is common. Only Y appears to be different.

It has been this way for a long time

That is where the mistake is. Since we start with this misunderstanding in the brain that we (X) are the body (Y), we as an imaginary entity suffer. That imaginary entity is Mary! See, there are only 2 things here: X, the feeling of Existence, which you feel strongly and the body Y, a muscular and skeletal mass, with the ability to think. But can you show me where Mary is? You cannot. Because it is just a thought. A thought repeated continuously throughout this birth.

This is not a mistake that happened this morning. For several *Janmas* (births) it has been there. So it is very hard to disassociate the nameless, formless eternal entity X that you are, from the body and this idea of a person. For e.g. Does the body say I am female, or do you see the body and say I am female? The body does not. In the next birth the body still won't say anything. But you will be saying I am male. So then, which is true? Male or Female? Just based on the outfit, the dress, you (X) are identifying yourself one way or another. As death nears you panic because you have identified the death of Y with the death of you (X). Also, there is a total boredom here. How many more times will you keep coming back in a cycle of birth, growth, marriage, fear, suffering, death? After a point it becomes stale. Hence your question or comment 'I don't want another birth'.

How to rectify it

So to know who you really are, you need to shift the attention from Y and focus on X. You know that Y came and will go soon. X alone will remain. But to experience X, the best time is when there is Y. Not before Y or after Y. Because to experience something it is easier to see it in relation to something else. For e.g. *Person A is short, makes sense only in relation to Person B who is tall, and vice versa.* So this is the best time to experience yourself. That is why a human birth is so important.

Now, this Knowing, this Understanding: Is it related to the physical body Y or to X? It is related to X. So, all we need is this understanding and knowing that I am X. There will be Y1, Y2, Y3 --- Yn. But X is only one. So forget about Y. You are not Y1... Yn. You are X. You as X take on Y1, Y2, etc. So understanding and experiencing X is the only way to attain freedom from association with Y1, Y2, etc. Knowing X is *Jnanam*. *Jnanam* is just another word for *Arivu*, Intelligence, Knowing. It is possible in a human body. That's why a human birth is so important. But sadly, all our efforts are towards knowing and satisfying what? Y. Not X. Tell me one thing you have done towards knowing X. Also, we don't know how long Y will last. It could end any time. Therefore, if you work really really hard in the time available to know X, to know yourself, it is possible.

The step to making this happen is the 'Guru-Disciple Relationship'. Know that Father, Mother, Wife, Husband are all relations merely tied to the body. As they (X) think they are the body (Y), they relate you to themselves as a body. But it is not a true relationship. These are mere assumptions. The same X in you, is the X in your husband, your daughter, etc. X is the same. But we see each as different because we are looking at Y. This is *Maya* (illusion). Seeing the same thing everywhere but mistaking it to be different things is *Maya*. If you are stuck in it, suffering is guaranteed. If you free yourself from *Maya*, then happiness is guaranteed. This freeing yourself from *Maya* is *Atma Jnanam*, Liberation.

Each one of us has the capability to free ourselves from *Maya*. But only some even have the thought or desire to free themselves. Only those who have matured over so many lives and have done many good deeds, only they get this thought, and finally they come in front of a Guru. This is the final relationship to destroy this identification of You with the Body and come out of this *Maya*. Guru is a new relationship. The final one. The one that sees you not as a body (Y) but as *Atma* (X). Surrendering everything to the Guru, living with him, and serving him should be how you spend the rest of your life. He knows where you are, where he needs to bring you, and what the steps are.

It comes down to your decision alone. Ask me what ever you need to ask. But once you make a decision, stick to it strongly. 'I must find out who I am'. That strong discipline you should have and be willing to grow.

I am waiting. Very happy to speak with you. *Nandri. Nandri. Nandri* (Thank you!) Gurudeva. [With these words Mahaprabu ended the Satsang]

Mahaprabu later said: These moments when a yearning soul comes to me with a sincere desire to come out of its suffering, these moments are the ones I live for. If THAT wishes, I will take how many ever *janmas* it takes, to free them. Even if I have to keep coming back till the last person is freed. As new disciples come, you (looking at us disciples) will also be impacted positively. *Just as when a mother of teenage children gives birth to a new child, with the coming of the child they will also become soft, just as the mother shows her softness to the child!*

Atma, Body, World

In my ignorance, I spoke with Sri Mahaprabu about how after sitting for a long meditation, I saw Existence as the space or substratum in which Thoughts arise, and the distinctions between Awareness and Thought. I was hoping to get affirmation from him. This was his response.

Mahaprabu: There should be no more analysis. That which you are trying to experience, is it something that can be got through thinking? *No.* It is beyond the mind. And all these analyses, who is it for? Is it for Existence? *No.* So we need to stop the thinking process as much as possible in order to begin to experience who we are.

There are only 3 things. There is the Body, the World and *Unarvu* (Feeling of Existence, Atma). The Body and World have a temporary existence. But *Unarvu* is:

a) Always there 24×7, Indestructible, Nameless, Formless: *Sat*

b) Is Knowing, is Aware: *Cit*

c) Is Peace: *Ananda*

Yet we don't give *Unarvu* any time or attention at all. And we don't realize that it is only this *Unarvu* that appears as a wife, son, father, friend, etc.

Now besides these 3 things, there is nothing. So where is GR? (referring to ego – my initials) He does not exist at all. Yet, he is the source of so many problems. True, the body and world give problems, but nowhere near the magnitude of the problems created by GR. The goal is to realize the absence of GR as much as possible and realize the *Unarvu*.

The basics

If you considered a timeline, this *Unarvu* existed before the birth of the body (call that period X), during life (call this period Y) and continues to exist after death (call this period Z). Only the body (call it B) comes and goes.

[Mahaprabu was driving to Thiruvannamalai, past midnight when he was explaining all this over the phone.]

Figure 1

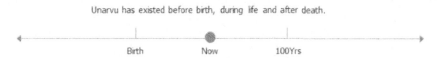

Unarvu has existed before birth, during life and after death.

Before birth (X) of body it exists
After death (Z) of body it will exist
During life (Y) it exists
Only body (B) comes and goes

Figure 2

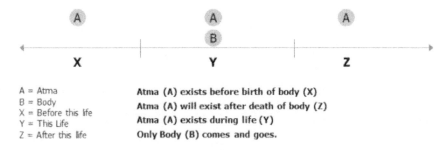

A = Atma
B = Body
X = Before this life
Y = This Life
Z = After this life

Atma (A) exists before birth of body (X)
Atma (A) will exist after death of body (Z)
Atma (A) exists during life (Y)
Only Body (B) comes and goes.

Do not worry or fear B.

A is the key.

Without A, B is nothing.

In both X and Z, you cannot even discriminate A vs. B, since B does not exist. Only in Y, you can even know that A exists separately. *Just like ice touching ice will not know what cold is. Only a warm body touching ice will know cold.*

Only in this birth of the body, is there a possibility to know A. So do not squander this opportunity. Also don't analyze the state before Y ie. X and Z. Because you will have to imagine things and can get cheated. Focus on Y alone. If you know A in Y, it is the same A in X and Z. (Laughing)

The Urgency of the Situation

Do not waste a single moment doing things such as the study of Vedanta, taking care of orphans, etc. First complete the task for which you are born, which is Self-Realization. Someone else will do the other tasks. Accidentally someone showed you the priority, just like a blind man is shown the way.

Even if you come back to another life you should come with the priority of Realization only. So focus on Realization first. Already more than 50% of life is wasted. This should be your attitude, 'Even if I am born, let me not forget you *Ātma*'. The *Unarvu,* the feeling of Existence in you, is the same as *Sat Cit Ananda,* which is *Ātma*, which is the same as God. First know the God in you, where you are established 24 hours, then worry about the rest. Everything else is a distraction only. The next 20 years are key. It will fly. Don't waste it. Be alert.

Create an outer and inner ambiance that is conducive to this effort. Give it top priority. Be without distractions both outside and inside. Stop unnecessary activities. *Doing them is like throwing heaps of garbage on a sapling.*

Learn to Live

Sri Mahaprabu pointed out how all of us are living life, totally forgetting who is in control. Thinking we are doing it all. He explained the mechanism of how IT creates, sustains and ends everything. Yet we say we are searching for God! Therefore, what should be our attitude as we live life each day that is given to us by that Creator? A fantastic conversation.

Creation is doing it

Mahaprabu was driving to Tiruvannamalai when he called me. It was near midnight. The topic moved toward how people are living their lives. He gave this example first. *An IAS collector (a prestigious role as a senior administrative official) goes through such a busy schedule throughout his day. But not even for a second does he stop to think about that which makes him breathe. (Laughing) Think about it. Morning to night he doesn't even think that he is breathing. Yet there is an entire process happening. 'If only air did not go into the body, would anyone call me a Collector? Will anyone respect me if that air didn't go?' He doesn't stop to think for even one second. That air because of which he is alive and respected, what respect does he give to that air? He won't even think of it.* In my view, he is not intelligent. Instead, he is a fool and a pitiable fellow. The whole life he goes on missing.

On the other hand, when we think that this air is going into our bodies all the time and making the entire body run, a) it is shocking b) there is a sense of gratitude and c) our minds become light. Something is taking care of the body. Why do we have to worry? We are in somebody's hands. If you understand this fact well, that you are totally in somebody's hands, then will you worry? No. Because you have forgotten this, there is worry. If only 100%, 1000%, 100,000% you realized you are in somebody's hands; He who gives you air, water, and heat, then will you worry? *Suriyan varuvadhu yaarale.* (Who makes the sun shine? Mahaprabu sang a couple of lines of this song that is usually part of the morning prayer.) Mahaprabu did not pick this song by accident. IT is running the whole thing. Also, it is not running everything like a machine. The difference between this and machines is that machines don't have love. This Supreme Power runs everything so well and it does it with love. It has made everything. Yes, we know how to mix this with that and create something different. But that brain also was created by God. He has been with us throughout. If we realized this, how would we live? Happily, smiling. If we get something we will say 'It is His grace'. If we didn't get it, we would say 'He didn't want us to have it'. So happy, either way.

That is why Mahaprabu wants you to remember the most gracious moment at least once a day. Just having an opportunity to do so is great. The more and more you do it, you will develop a great love for the Creator. You will realize that everything is created by Him, and also taken care of by Him. Then you will simply travel happily. You will be In the Journey. Everyone says and thinks 'Journey towards God'. Instead, it should be 'Journey with God'. Just be with him.

GR: Yes, a journey towards God implies we know where he is. With God means, we go wherever he goes, he takes us.

What a lie 'Searching for God' is

Look at how big this earth is. Did you create it? Did your dad or mom create it? Just go to the terrace and sit down. Then look at the vast sky and then the earth for 15 minutes. You will peacefully come down, eat and sleep. Will you then search for God? You will not. Search only comes when something has disappeared. Or if you are not able to see it you will search. But looking at the sky and earth for 15 minutes can you say you can't see God?

GR: I'm doing almost that Mahaprabu. Looking at the sky, eating and sleeping.

Mahaprabu: Yes, very good, *jollya pannu*. Do it happily.

GR: That's hard to do.

Mahaprabu: Yes, so who makes it difficult for you? God or your thoughts?

GR: Definitely my thoughts!

Mahaprabu: See how it tortures you. It doesn't let you be. Actually you can be very happy. This is what your practice should be. Learn to Live. Not learn to do *Dhyanam* etc. Just as in learning to drive, you be with someone who drives, or to swim you be with someone who swims, to learn to live, be with Mahaprabu as he knows how to live. *Vaaza Pazagu.* Learn to Live. Just go to the terrace and look at the sky and earth. Your dad or my dad didn't create it. All this is proof that He exists. Aren't His creations proof that He exists? Then why are you searching? See what a big lie, 'searching' is. He is one who can be felt everywhere, not seen. He is hiding behind all his creations. You can see the sky and the earth. We didn't create them. So he must have created them. That's more than enough evidence. Then why are you searching? Laughing...

It's like this. *Say, you always wear your slippers when you leave your house. You never go out barefoot. Someone comes to your house and sees your slippers outside the door. What will he think?* GR: That I'm home! Mahaprabu: Yes! (Laughing). That's all. With such a small thing as slippers, he believes and decides that you are home. Such a big earth, such a big sky! And you keep on searching for God. He is there. He is behind His creations; he is AS His creations. He is the creation, He is the power that creates, the intelligence that creates. We also are His creations. He is behind everything and in every thing. He can be felt. He is not something that can be seen because all that is seen are His creations. The one that is seeing itself, is His creation. *Padaippa irukkaru. Unara kudiya amsama irrukkaru.* He is creation itself. He is something that can be experienced.

The mechanism

Buddha found this first. He said, first observe the air that is going into your nose. As you observe this very closely for a long time you will learn a lot about it.

Does the air go into you because your lungs suck it in?

GR: The Lungs help suck it in.

Mahaprabu: Are the lungs enough? Then why doesn't a dead body with a fresh young set of lungs not suck it in? Take a 20-year-old boy. Won't his lungs be good? Yes. He went to bed. At 6 AM, some valve in his heart stopped working and he died. At 6:05 they found out. So, weren't the lungs there at 6:05? Air is around and has been around. At 5:55, the air stopped going in. That's why the valve stopped working. What happened is, that the *prapancham* (universe) decided to stop sending air in at 5:55 AM.

GR: Wow, so you are saying that the cause for breathing is outside.

Mahaprabu: Yes, that's exactly what I'm saying. Take a balloon. How will you pump air into it. Assume there is a pump that can push air into it, and suck air out of it. A two-way pump. When you pump once the balloon will inflate. When you pump again, it will deflate. Our body is the same. Lungs are the balloon. Atmosphere is the pump. (Laughing) The balloon is working because of the pump. The pump is not working because of the balloon. Similarly, the body is functioning because of the air around it!! Only the air makes the lungs work. The balloon by itself cannot suck air into itself nor send it out. Similarly, there is a formless pump outside. It is the main pump. Your lungs, heart, etc. are all secondary pumps, a sub-assembly. They can't survive a second without the main pump, which is outside. Think, the whole atmosphere has air, and lungs are ready in a dead body, but the air does not go in!

See how perfectly it works. When it decides, it says 'Today at this time air will stop being sent into this body.' Not just humans. Insects, dogs, cows, all of it. A very big system is working. The tiny human mind cannot fathom it. *Take someone new to Chennai on a tour throughout Chennai to various parts and drop him back at Kodambakkam. Then ask him to retrace the route. He won't be able to. Places he just visited an hour ago he won't be able to go there again.* So limited is the human brain. Can it figure out creation?

There is no door to the body. Nostrils are always open. Lungs are there. Pump (atmosphere) is always there. Life force (call it bio-electricity) goes through the air only. That's why when you close the nose and mouth of someone they will die. Or if you immerse him in water he will die. Yet, fish and so many water creatures get their life force only in that same water. Leave them outside water and they struggle to death. See how beautifully it creates.

GR: How about accidental death Mahaprabu? Isn't that also from outside?

Mahaprabu: Yes! Everything is controlled down to the second. All IT has to do is say *Konja vegamma vottu.* Please drive fast now! (we both burst out laughing!). That's all it takes to end someone's life. Make someone else drive fast! Forget about accidents. It can even say, tomorrow morning you must hang yourself. And the man wakes up ties the noose and hangs himself! No one else told him. Think! For e.g. If I tell you to hang yourself, will you? Can anyone make someone hang from a noose? (Laughing) His own thoughts say it to him. Who is making this happen?

How to live

Mahaprabu: See how all are living like fools. At least if they lived as fools that would be tolerable. Worse, they think they are so brilliant. That's what makes it so pitiable. For example, *A total beggar is there. But he thinks that he is a king, and is sitting on the road thinking he is a king!* This needs to be taught to people. This is Enlightenment. Nothing else.

GR: You are right Mahaprabu. That's all we need to do. But we are unable to stay quiet, sit quietly.

Mahaprabu: Yes. You have to keep on going towards God with love. Then he will make you sit quietly. But you are not sitting for him (referring to meditation). You are sitting for yourself. That's why he keeps on waking you up! (Burst out laughing). *Yezuppi, Yezuppi vudaraaru vunna.*

GR: You are so right. I'm sitting not out of love for him, but to gain something.

Mahaprabu: Yes! (continuing the prayer song) *Yedho yengo irrukiradhe. Yaaro yengo irrupadhu mei. Andha porulai naam ninaithe...* (Something somewhere exists. Let us think of that.) Do we think about IT? If 100% you realize you are in someone's hands totally, from there alone does real joy start. Real life begins there. The end of imagination. End of an imaginary life.

So live very happily. Only 2 things you can do for now. *Prarthanai* (Prayer) or *Nandri Sollu* (have Gratitude). Why do you need intelligence? Just have enough intelligence to know you are a fool. Just knowing you are a beggar is enough. You don't need to know much else. That's all you need to know. That you are a fool. You have been living as though you are so intelligent. This is Realization. Knowing that you have been doing a foolish thing.

So just learn to be peaceful. But as long as 'you' are there, it won't let you be peaceful. Truth is ever-present. The lie is temporary. It keeps on changing. The lie won't let you sit for long. That's why it won't let you sit quietly. You aren't real. *Irai Sakthi dhaan unmai.* God alone is real. Only a few days are left. Keep on thinking of the *Padaicha Sakthi* (the Creator). Look at you. You have everything. No one is going to call you and say 'Why are you idle?' No one has that right. Yet does it let you stay quiet? No. See how careful you need to be. You have to learn to Be. *Irukka Pazagu.* Learn to be. *Iraiva Nandri.* Thank you God. I'm seeing you in all your creations.

For example, *a man is living with his granddaughter who looks exactly like the mother (his daughter) who is living abroad. The daughter calls and says how are you, you must be missing me. He says, 'No. I'm seeing you every day, every minute, in your daughter.' Think! He will be seeing his granddaughter (Sunita) but will be thinking about his daughter (Anita). Just for example.* Like this we should learn to enjoy God's creation every minute. Through the creations, feel God. Just like the granddaughter is the creation of his daughter. While touching her he says, your nose is just like your mother's! The Creator might not be near but his creations are so near. This is what our time should be spent on. Instead, if you focus on consciousness, super consciousness.... Laughing... There is no meaning. Whatever time is left, use it for this. Be happy. *Magizchiya iru,* Be happy, joyful. *Magizchiye avarudaya padaippu dhan,* Joy itself is His creation. Do you see sadness somewhere? Sadness is his creation also. Do you see *Kama* (desire, lust) anywhere? *Kama* is his creation too. Has anyone barred you from living this way?

So much guilt has been built up around *Kama*. I ask you, aren't all children of one source, the Mother? *Yellam oru thai makkal* (all are from one Mother alone). So then all are your brothers and sisters. Who will you have sex with? You can't even touch your wife. You can't have a relationship with anyone. Then why are all those organs produced? We are the ones who separate things as good and bad e.g., Sex is bad.

If only you saw everything and everyone as God's creations, all your mind's impurities would be washed away over time. Everything will come to a neutral. Right now there are so many ups and downs in the ground of your mind. It will become level as though a bulldozer went over it.

Romba Magizchi. Romba Magizchi. Be Happy.

If it is a dream why bother?

A common trap for a seeker is to claim that it is all a dream, everything is an illusion, so why bother trying to improve? All efforts are in the dream etc. Sri Mahaprabu shatters this misconception by giving a clear picture of what is actually going on.

GR: The world definitely seems like a figment of imagination, with various dream personalities. So, why should I strive for perfection for GR (Initials of disciple and refers to the ego. Substitute your initials here): if he is fiction, in a dream? I mean why perfect him from Kama, Krodha, etc? (Referring to the 6 enemies of desire, anger, greed, pride, attachment and delusion). It leads to suppression and guilt. Why bother fixing him if the whole thing is a dream?

Mahaprabu: Your understanding is good. But be careful. GR is entirely Thought. But Kama (desire, lust, etc) has a Body aspect, a Thought aspect, and a Unarvu (Feeling) aspect. GR himself could be pretending as Awareness! He will split into two. Normal GR (Let's call it NGR) and Spiritual GR (Let's call it SGR). NGR has Kama Vasanas. SGR opposes it. But SGR is actually NGR. NGR does not want SGR to oppose him. So a 3rd role is created by NGR (Mahaprabu was laughing) where NGR pretending as SGR becomes a referee: Let's call him HGR – Hybrid!! Who will he side with? He will tilt the game toward NGR! This HGR will appear to treat both sides as equal but eventually will side NGR's way. In fact, SGR is created by NGR for the very purpose of getting his way. GR wins in the end! (Peals of laughter)

Surrendering is the only way

Surrender means getting rid of all 3. No games. Surrender all these thoughts of 'It is a dream' etc. Only live as a Disciple. I belong to Him (Guru). I am here on His terms. In every act bring in the feel of: 'On behalf of Him I am here, I am doing it for Him'. This is Awareness. Slowly progress. Cooperation will increase. At the point, when you say 'On behalf of', you are creating Awareness and pulling Mahaprabu. Uyir (Life Source) is contacting Uyir, so the connection will happen. Energy will come to you from here, which will push you ahead. At that point, due to the connection, a solution to a specific situation will also come from Mahaprabu and it will be the right decision. *Yennagalaal erpatta ninaipu, anmai connectiona marum:* What began as a thought will transform into a connection at the level of Atma.

GR: Should I invoke the physical form of Mahaprabu?

Mahaprabu: Yes. That is all you can do. The transformation will take it from Physical -> Mental -> Spiritual. If you try to do it yourself, it means you have again put on the SGR role for Guru! (Laughing). So SGR is definitely coming!! (Laughing).

This is beyond mind. The Supreme Power is directly speaking with you. It is giving you a clear picture. The Supreme Power is operating through Mahaprabu. Make this your attitude: I surrender to that intelligence, the Supreme Power which is beyond mental intelligence. Now that I understand this, I need to implement it.

Take a strong decision and be strong in that decision. (referring to the decision to Surrender)

About Meditation

Sri Mahaprabu has never taught meditation as a technique. 'Techniques are for the mind. The meditator is the one that needs to disappear' he says. And 'Not even meditation is needed for *Unarvu* (Feeling of Existence) to exist. Only IT exists.' And 'Putting an effort to Meditate is like coming out of one's home and starting to search for it.' Nevertheless, he continuously stresses the need to sit down for long stretches of time and just feel your Existence. Nothing else.

These are a collection of messages from Sri Mahaprabu at various times, regarding the topic of Meditation.

Why Sitting is important

Sri Mahaprabu once again used letters to simplify his explanation of why one has to make the body sit.

X = Physical Body.

Y = Flow of Thoughts.

Speed of Y is > X.

X is operated by Y. When both move, you don't notice the speed.

When Sitting, speed of X = zero. Now the speed of Y is felt.

The goal is to bring Y to zero.

For this, X needs to be brought to zero.

Eventually, Y will be zero even when X is moving.

First, get the body used to Sitting

Get the body used to sitting. Five times a day. An hour each time. Poor body. It has no say. It is dumb. The mind takes it for a ride. And when it can't take it for a ride, then the mind goes anyway. For example, it can go to India now, just by thought. *So, the mind is the bird that can take its nest (the body) anywhere. What you have to do first is to anchor the nest. The mind will try and try but one day it will give up. It is now restricted to a large extent. That will be a huge advancement.*

And all sitting sessions won't be the same. Out of 7 days x 5 times, only one day might be good. That is enough! *It takes several attempts but only 1 sperm creates the egg.* But all those other efforts are necessary. Therefore, stopping the body (the nest), then stopping the mind (the bird) is needed to warm and hatch the egg of enlightenment!

How Sitting helps

Make the body sit. While sitting, You and Thoughts exist. Then Thoughts decrease. *Nee mattum Iruppa,* You alone are. This 'I alone AM' will give you a new experience. Attention will go on that. As you start getting used to ignoring the mind, it will lose its hold on you. So keep on sitting for Dhyanam regularly. The mind will resist. But after a few tries, it will give up resisting. 'IT' will take over. An understanding will come. After that, you have no control. It is like *bringing a horse to the edge of the river and pushing its head into the water. The drinking will happen automatically.*

Why do we insist on sitting in Meditation? (as opposed to walking or running). When you sit and 'you' are not there, there will be an experience. That experience teaches you that it is not the posture, rather it is your absence that causes the experiences. Because at the time of the experience, the body will not be in your conscious. So, YOU NOT THERE leads to EXPERIENCE. Not the posture. This you will get initially only when you sit. Since you've been running all along (body with mind) 'you' think that running means you can't lose yourself and sitting is the only way. That is why 'you' make the body sit. It is a misunderstanding. The lack of struggle when you sit and be present is due to the lack of 'you'. Not because of sitting. But based on past data and seeing so many seekers and saints you have programmed in you the guidelines that to be in that state one must sit. Posture does not matter. But initially, it helps.

Increase the frequency and duration of meditation. And practicing Awareness during the day will strengthen the ability to sit for a longer time in meditation. Only while sitting you will see the Truth. Only practicing during the day with Presence will make sitting possible. Create an environment and mental framework for sitting down.

Your target is 5 times a day of sitting.

Set the mind for sitting five times a day. One hour of sitting plus two hours of free time. Like this five times during the day. 6 hours of sleep. Plan your schedule accordingly for those two-hour gaps. (These instructions were for me, given my life situation. For those who work during the day he the instructions are modified) Only if you do this, Ātma will let GR go (GR refers to ego. Substitute your initials here.) Right now it is a mental understanding. Next, a spiritual understanding is needed. Since the poison is at the spirit level. Then a final decision will come to drop GR. Only then Ātma will decide to drop GR. Once he decides to drop, the movement is faster.

Don't sit for meditation with expectation

It is a universal need of the mind to find something better than the present. You are always interested in knowing if there is something more interesting than this. In summary, the belief is that the moment which will make me happy is somewhere in the future and somewhere else. This is the expectation. But behind this is the biggest foolishness or ignorance. Because IT is always here and now.

Start from the point of I don't know. Acceptance of the experience is the way. In meditation, develop the attitude of accepting with an open mind. 'I don't know anything. I am here to observe.' Let there be interest, but not expectation. Don't sit for meditation in order to attain. Go inside to know. *Like an objective scientist. He does not know what he is going to find, so he observes carefully.* Watch where it takes you.

Don't get stuck to experiences in Meditation.

Don't go in looking for experiences, either new or ones that you had earlier. While going in don't hold on to anything. Let go and dive in. It is like, *you want to jump into a well for a nice swim, but you are holding onto the wall. You want to enjoy the water. But then why are you holding on to the wall? It is meaningless. (Laughing.)*

So don't hold on to anything. If in Dhyanam you are paying attention to experiences or expecting something, that is not going to help you. Attachment is not just outside. Inside too. You can easily become attached to your inner experiences.

Keep bringing the attention

In small things bring your attention to your Existence. Feel your Existence as you perform small tasks. Make all else unimportant. This decision brings a Total Surrender in you. That Surrender brings about an inner transformation. Take a strong pledge that hereafter I will not do anything without this inner contact. Whatever I do, first I will bring this inner contact. Only then will I focus on the task. Even if I am meeting with the President or God.

You have to work hard and you can work hard. Have faith in my words. Start your practice immediately. Come to a point where this practice is alone important. Only if you can stay in this state for a long time, only then something can happen inside. This decision and standing on this decision is the key to happiness.

The futility of Attempts

[After some duration, there was a time when I was frustrated that I was not progressing in the sense, I wasn't feeling a resulting joy, the *Ananda*, and complained about it to Sri Mahaprabu. He laughed.]

So, whenever you are making an attempt to meditate you should NOT make the attempt. Because meditation is always happening. Your attempts are getting in the way. But when will that happen? Only after so many attempts have been made. (laughing!)

Only after making so many attempts, you will reach a point of not making attempts. That is how the mind is. Even though you don't get *Ātma Jnāna* (enlightened) it will satisfy you that you have made attempts! See, because you made attempts, you learned that *Ananda* (bliss or peace) can't be found by looking for it. But if you did not make that attempt, will you have got this clarity? No!!

It is like this: *Let's say for example that you are a beggar with absolutely no food left to eat. By staying home, you will not get anything for sure. Only by begging, there is even an opportunity possible. You might not get it the first several times but one day you WILL get it. Unknown to you some person will happen to pass by that street you are begging in and simply give it to you and go.* Similarly, you have to try it in different ways till it CLICKS. The 'so many attempts' will make it click even though the attempts themselves didn't give it to you. It cannot be avoided. It is the process of ripening.

Surrender is the way

Bhagavan initiated self-enquiry for all beginners and visitors, but for those who surrendered to him, he attended to them very closely. An example is Annamalai Swami. He came to the ashram to sit and do meditation but Bhagavan made him work in construction for 9 long years. The difference was that the Guru was with him all along. Where the disciple is, the Master is. Once the disciple follows the Guru's words, Guru will follow the disciple.

Bhagavan Ramana Maharshi himself wrote in Ulladu Narpadu Anubandam: *When you get associated with your Master, the attachments in you will go away.*

All other relations will be cut. When this happens, the association with your ego will break. Thus detached from ego, mind, and identity they will find themselves in that eternal peace; unoscillating state. So, develop a strong relationship with the Guru.

Bhagavan also said *'Everyone indeed wants to attain moksha, but when I say "Give yourself unto me" they are unwilling to comply. Then how will moksha be attained?'*

See, there is no mention of enquiry, meditation, etc. in this message. Why should one associate with the Guru? Because Surrender will happen. Only there will you lose your ego, the decision-maker. Then an emptiness will happen which is the real transformation.

Meditator, Seeker are all only roles

Existence is not an idea. Meditation is an idea. And so Meditator is also just an idea too. That Existence is existing, has existed and will exist without the idea of a Meditator.

The role of a Disciple is the last one. Once you have become a disciple, the Master will not let you play the role of Meditator or Seeker. Meditator comes before Disciple. Because Meditator and Seeker are all ideas. I have to lose the role/idea of Seeker, Meditator. Disciple is NOT a better Meditator. It is an evolution. A Seeker or Meditator can become a Disciple. The Master will not allow me to play any role besides Disciple, and finally not even the role of Disciple either. Finally, at the nothingness of Ego, the fullness of Existence reveals itself. Without the knowledge of the Disciple, this will happen. It is an Evolution.

It is like this: *So far you have been flying in the air. Now you are driving a car on the road, but think you are flying, and are therefore driving in fear.* Fear can't be denied. Until you are Realized, this fear will continue. The Guru plays the role of the passenger in your car, and sympathizes with your fears, even though he knows that we are actually safe on the ground. He plays the role so that the disciple accepts the Master as the Guru.

Continuous Effort – Not just in Meditation

Master is always aware and in a training mindset 24×7, each and every moment. This is why just being in the presence of the Master, near him is enough. It is needed. *Like a poor boy who saves a few coins daily, becomes rich eventually.* Similarly bringing awareness and meditating constantly is needed because habits are so ingrained. *Like breaking branches of a big tree. Some come off easily. Some are so flexible that every fiber has to be twisted and ripped one after the other till the branch drops.* Similarly, continuous effort is needed for the mind also. If you bring awareness continuously without giving any gap then the detachment will happen. Detachment from the world, detachment from the body and detachment from 'i' will happen.

Only if you put in continuous effort, you will obtain the effortless State continuously. The main thing is continuity. That's why continuous effort is needed. When you think, walk, move, talk. Because even a single thought has a ripple effect. So, every moment you must be aware. *It is like there are two taps for water you can drink from at any time: One with dirty water and one with clean water. You must be careful which tap you are opening and drinking from.*

Take time during the day to sit, close your eyes and review how the day went so far. Where did we commit mistakes? What is our true nature? Then in the day-to-day activity this must consciously be corrected. That is Dhyanam. Otherwise, you will easily get addicted to sitting in meditation. It can become almost an irrecoverable addiction. Getting used to a routine and sitting in Dhyanam, inertia will set in. Similarly, one who's always active also has inertia as it is hard to make him sit. Your meditation should not depend on whether you're sitting or not. It is in no way related. If THAT wants to make the body sit, the body will obey and sit (the brain obeys and coordinates). When THAT wants the body to move, the brain will simply obey and carry it out. Right now, a third entity has come in the way. The mind. This drives the body. When it says sit you are sitting. When it says move you are moving. This also looks like a natural flow but you are deceived. Until you shift from this to THAT, a Master is needed.

Mahaprabu never teaches Meditation

Nobody can teach meditation. First understand that. It is not an act. It is a state which is happening each and every moment, always. It alone is existing. All other things are existing based on this permanent Existence. Through everything what is flowing? Meditation is flowing.

Mahaprabu can help you build the attitude in which you can come in touch with this Meditation that is always happening. Techniques will not work. When you follow techniques, you are relying on remembering it. Techniques are what? Shortcuts. To reduce time. So after meditation with technique, what will you do? You'll need tremendous patience to stay there. Then which technique will teach you patience? Patience cannot be a technique because all techniques are for those who are not patient! All kinds of techniques are used by whom? The mind only. By techniques the mind is not destroyed.

So a real Master always insists on the right attitude. He will ask you to develop the right attitude i.e. Keeping patient, doing everything without a hurry. Techniques are for the mind, Attitudes belong to the heart. No technique can give you love, which comes from the heart. All techniques are used for the external world. If you still want a technique, then tell your mind Yes here is your technique: "No more techniques". Let it go off and follow that.

Note: Sri Mahaprabu always reminds us, every single time, to do things with Awareness, slowly, without rush. *Thodarboda* (with contact with your feeling of Existence), *Porumaiya* (without rush) are the words we hear again and again. Over time, in his presence, we tend to naturally slow down.

If only we could remember this one thing

In every living organism there is a common thing. That is not made of bone or flesh. Behind the bone and flesh and blood, definitely something is existing which has no name, no form, which has the feeling of its own Existence and it knows that it is Existing, and in whose presence the organism lives and functions. The same thing is existing in ALL living beings. This you need to remember. That's all. This is the sadhana. If you remember this, it is enough. It is also in non-living beings but in a different state, where it is static, passive, not dynamic as in living things.

First remember continuously that something exists behind the bone, flesh and blood that has a feeling of Existence, knows it Exists and is formless. This is in all beings. This feeling, this remembrance we should have throughout the day. This must be your deepest practice. Not forgetting this is the sadhana.

It is a simple fact to remember. But even this simple thing we are unable to do. As this is the case, think about how strong the mind is. Think about how weak we are, and how much strength we need to build to remember this simple fact, throughout the day. This strength can be built through meditation, through Devotion, through Satsang, through Parayanam (chanting divine songs), through Surrender. All these things collectively help us develop the strength to keep remembering this simple fact. Not forgetting this is the Sadhana. If you do this, it is over.

So, find out why you aren't remembering it. Where are you missing it? What should you do to make sure you don't miss it? That's all.

The easiest way is Bhakti

The easiest way is through Devotion, Bhakti. Keep on thanking the creator. Surrender to Him totally. Before you sit for Meditation immerse yourself in Irai Bhakthi (devotion to God) or Guru Bhakti (devotion to Guru). Let that be the foundation. Then it will turn into Dhyanam effortlessly.

This is why we sing devotional songs. The heart can melt easily as you sing. As you melt in devotion, then when you sit for Dhyanam (meditation) you will enter into it effortlessly. *It is like priming the pump. Before pumping water out of the ground, they first pour a little bit of water into the pump and give it a few hard pushes. Then the water starts to flow easily.* Similarly, start with devotion. Try it and see for yourself. [GR: I have been practicing this for some time now and it is the only way I can meditate anymore.]

Or if you cannot sing, practice Omkaram (chanting of Om). And don't chant it mechanically. Om is the sound of God. Chant it with love. You are welcoming the Supreme Power. Then see what should be the quality of that chant! Give it everything you have. At least 15 to 30 minutes you must chant. Then you can easily glide into meditation. [During Satsang we often do Omkaram with Sri Mahaprabu. He chants Om and we repeat. It is nearly impossible to keep up with his level of chanting but we try. It has a tremendous effect on the meditation that follows immediately. An hour goes by without much notice.]

So when you melt in devotion by singing or chanting, Meditation comes to you easily. Because God is with you now. And what is it you are seeking? God! So he will take care of you. You don't need to do anything. Instead what people are doing? OK. It is 6 o'clock. I am going to sit and meditate. You start with a technique. And you expect things to happen. As though God was waiting for you to start. (Laughing).

The Cause of Worry

Mentioned to Mahaprabu that sometimes I go into this Worry-Loop, a kind of heavy feeling and it takes time to come out of it. Most often the cause is that I am not putting to practice the teachings, especially the 'be aware, be in the present moment' teaching. This was his response.

What gives that heavy feeling?

So many things inside the body are happening automatically. Therefore collectively the body is operating automatically. During day-to-day activities it is good to feel the substratum (Feeling of Existence). You will experience it as though you are a leaf freely blowing in the wind. As you feel the substratum more and more, the idea of an individual will eventually come to zero. The absence of mind is seen. The body will function externally also automatically. Mahaprabu's body is very light. Sometimes he does not know if it is even there or not. Thought is the one that is heavy. That is why lazy people are created. Since their thoughts are heavy, they can't function well.

GR: When interacting with people, the substratum, awareness is dormant.

Mahaprabu: Since identification with the Ego is strong. *Ice caps may be strong but the sun has begun rising. They won't melt at 6 am. It will take time.* Don't worry. Instead, feel the joy when you are aware again. Tell the ego: You have played your role. Do your thing but your time of expiry has started. That should be the attitude.

Worry leads to Tamoguna

Worry is bad. It leads to Tamoguna. You will eat, shout, sleep, TV, look for sex etc. Don't worry that you are not Aware. Accept that due to identification with Ego, that incident happened. Counsel yourself that learning has started. Years, Janmas of bad habit is the cause, but the End is near. Guru always forgives. Guru sees only one thing in a disciple: Is he sincere in getting rid of ignorance.

Accept that you know only all this intellectually. Only now you're starting to practice. All this can happen when we are courageous and 'encourageous' to ourself. So try the opposite when you are worried. Instead of worrying about slipping on ice, rejoice over the Sunrise! Practice consistently. Have faith. GR is fake. Ātma is real. Under any circumstance don't lose this faith. This attitude is very essential to progress. Satsang will help, like a float or life vest. Laugh at yourself. Make it a fun game. Enlightenment as a goal should be joyful. Enjoy the path. It's like this: *Two people enter a forest. One is extremely nervous and fears every step. The other person enjoys nature at every step and is happy. Who would have had a better experience traveling through the forest?*

Only high-ego people are enlightened

Don't worry. No one is going to hang you. *Poradhe Varadhukaga thane* (Your leaving awareness is only to come back!). Due to impatience and expectation of immediate results we worry. Tremendous patience is needed. Like a pendulum. And the more the Ego, the more the swing. The high ego person suffers the consequences of his ego tremendously (goes to one extreme) and that suffering drives him to conquer it (goes to the other extreme). This is why high-ego people are enlightened. Only they are eligible. Ordinary people cannot enter. When Mahaprabu meets a seeker, he is able to scan them. The Jnani will still accept the low ego seeker, but he will actually work on developing their ego! He knows. Only a professional builder can destroy a building well!

Keep on practicing

Keep on practicing awareness. Thank it. The sun is rising. Keep encouraging yourself. With high-energy and tremendous patience go forward. Substratum/Ātman is there. Body is there. World is there. No GR. Without GR this existence has existed. GR is purely imaginary!

When you convert these understandings into practice you will experience it.

Failing to Surrender

On the way to spending a few weeks with Sri Mahaprabu I decided to first go to the Himalayas and spend 3 days in solitude. All plans were made for travel and stay. But at the last minute, very strange circumstances prevented me from taking the detour and I ended up straight at the Resthouse with Mahaprabu. He spoke to me then.

Feeling towards Guru

Mahaprabu: There is a primary ignorance that I am a human being. Clearly there was a time when people did not know they were humans. Yet, they had a feeling of their Existence. That same Existence feeling is still there today. But they felt it more than us. This is because today, the 'I am a human' thought masks it. Is this thought necessary?

Going to special places or pilgrimages only strengthens it. Once you have surrendered, planning should not be there for you. Surrender means body, mind, and Spirit have been surrendered. While you were describing your intentions for the trip, I could feel a strong No. Since you did not ask Sri Mahaprabu's permission, nature intervened in various forms. If you had asked Mahaprabu, I would have said No. But surrender still worked! Guru's energy will help you make the right move. By thinking of Guru as a mere name and form, your energy is limited because the opening in you is small. But when you think of him as a Supreme Power, even though it is a thought, you will find a larger opening in you. In fact, it is the Supreme Power in you that is opening up. Therefore, the *Unarvu* (feeling) of Guru as a Supreme Power is good for you.

SC (Sri Mahaprabu gave me the name Satchitanandam. Henceforth no GR): The mind moves towards unimportant things even though I understand well in theory that it is the wrong thing.

Mahaprabu: For example, *a great leader, say a president, might have thousands of employees but it is impossible for him to know each one of them. That is why they have a hierarchy from top to bottom where each layer knows the layer below.* But it is not like that with the Guru. Whoever thinks of the Guru, whether or not the Guru thinks about him they are blessed. They are connected. You are connected to Mahaprabu. That's why even though you did not tell him you were going, nature intervened since you had signed the 'MOU' (using Memorandum of Understanding as a metaphor). Similarly, Mahaprabu also has signed the MOU, that at all times, without expecting anything in return, without compromising your situation, his only goal is moving you towards enlightenment. You might violate your side of the agreement, but Mahaprabu will never.

More on Surrender

Spend every minute with Mahaprabu, as much as you can. You are coming to Chennai. Spend maximum time with Guru when you are there.

SC: Yes, this was my intention and I knew it conflicted with my desire to be in solitude on the banks of the Ganges.

Mahaprabu: Nature has guided you to the Master. You have found water in a place. Will you not continue to dig there? Only then will you add to what you have got. Instead, will you move away and try somewhere else, and then somewhere else? You don't have much time. Use it vigorously. At every instant think of the Guru. That's why in earlier days they had Nāmāvali (chanting various names of God, e.g., 108 names of Shiva etc.) so that God would always be in the mind of the chanter. Always think: Mahaprabu is with me. I am only here in this earth for Jnānam. Only for that, each day has been given to me. For me to learn that I am the nameless, formless being.

You have only two choices: a) You can take on more janmās and add to your karmās or b) Leave all your karmās and return home by attaining Jnāna. Wealth, relations, study of books, none of these got you happiness this far. Mahaprabu is trying to wake you up. He came in your way and stopped you from going in that same direction, e.g. East, and made you turn Westward. You need a strong decision sense, that you will no longer go back East, because if you do, you will have to track backwards, all those steps. Mahaprabu knows what is East and what is West, because he also at one point was traveling East.

On Mahaprabu's behalf watch nature every minute. You are already attained. You don't need to gain Ātma. You only need to lose your false identity.

Constantly yearn to serve the Guru

Stay with Mahaprabu. Think about how to Serve Him. That thought itself will unite you with him. Opportunities for service will open up. (SC lives very far away physically from Chennai). *For example, a boy A yearns for girl B and tries to woo her really hard. But B is not interested. He does not get B, but in the end gets another girl C without any effort. Here C was the right choice for him. All his efforts for B would not have gotten him B, but those efforts will never go to waste. It is those efforts that got him C!* Therefore, it is the yearning that is important and not the person!

Similarly, yearning to serve the Guru is important. Those who long for it will get the opportunity. In that yearning, Surrender goes up and ego goes down. Service to the Guru leads to spiritual maturity. Therefore, the first step is yearning to serve the Guru. Forget trying to attain Ātma. It is already attained. Try to lose yourself. And where can you do that? Only at the feet of the Master. That is why Surrender is strongly recommended.

Note: 3 years have passed since this conversation happened. I am so grateful for everything that has happened through the Guru. Every word he said back then still rings true, fresh and fragrant as ever.

Pain and Pleasure Explained

Sri Mahaprabu explains in amazing depth, what Pleasure and Pain are. Do they have any existence? Who feels them? What is the result? He shows how these two phenomena keep us oscillating throughout our lives, never allowing us to be on steady ground. And as always, he points us to the solution. How to come out of this.

Who undergoes all this suffering? Has Existence suffered because of the body? No. Has the body suffered because of Existence? The body has very minimal suffering and it is taken care of by Existence. That is why aches and pains don't last long. No, neither Existence nor the body suffers really. It is the SC in between (SC refers to Ego. Put your initials here.) And what use is SC? The body itself belongs to Existence which takes care of it. So what is SC there for? Nothing.

Pain

Take a cut or a wound. Is the pain felt by the muscles? No. So the body itself does not feel pain. What is Pain? Pain is something that is defined by an entity which is related to the body. Let us say that at 9 PM you have a cut on your leg. You don't take any medication. Just let it be. There is pain, but who feels it? Not the body, because at midnight in deep sleep the same pain should be felt if it is the body that feels pain. Who are all there in deep sleep? Existence, the Body along with the Cut. Yet none of them give any information or complaints about pain. But on waking, the pain is felt. By whom? Pain is felt by the Ego alone. Let us see how.

X
BODY
Has Cut
No Pain

Y
EGO
No Cut
Has Pain

Z
EXISTENCE
No Cut
No Pain

Y shouldn't have pain since he doesn't have the cut. Then is the pain true? No! Pain is false. The cut is somewhere else! *It is like someone slapped your neighbor but your cheek swells up each time.* What brings Pain, is a record of it. That's all. Meaning, an impression is formed that if the eyes see such a cut, if it is bleeding, etc, then it should hurt. So Pain is a mental record, not a true phenomenon.

Pleasure

Pleasure also works exactly the same way. The entity that feels the pleasure (Y) is not where the object was experienced (X or Z). Pleasure is not in the sweet that is consumed. This is the Maya. By constant repetition to ourselves and our children that if it is like this it is pain, if it is like that it is pleasure, we have made an innocent child deluded by pain and pleasure. The whole life is trapped in these 2 records. Pleasure makes you feel like you hit the sky. Pain makes you feel like you are in a hole. And the worst part is that when you are down with pain, you want to go high up with pleasure instead of coming back to a neutral state of Being. This is Maya. And pleasure in turn always ends where? In Pain! As a result, you are never on the ground, steady, peaceful, unoscillating. You are going up and down, up and down.

How to escape from Pain and Pleasure

You have to come out of the Pain and Pleasure trap. When they rise, Vizhippu Unarvu (Awareness feeling) must rise. An Awareness machine must be running inside you constantly. For starters only for a short while, but keep increasing it. It has the capacity to go on for 24 hours. Only then a full understanding will happen. The rise of Pleasure and Pain will disappear, and you will be free.

When do you suffer? Only when Vizhippu Unarvu is absent. For example, there are many levels of pain, Less, Medium, High, etc. but they are all just mental records. Still, when you are in pain, it is too late to have the Awareness. It won't happen. Pain will stamp you out. Similarly, Pleasure will come suddenly. You will miss the inner Guru and therefore miss the outer Guru also.

So, have a very clear understanding that Pain and Pleasure are both false; Only the record of them is true, So we don't need to delete Pain and Pleasure, just delete the record! The record alone is true. Actually there is no existence of Pain or Pleasure. But you don't know when these 2 will arise and at what level they are in you. You can't plan for it. You will keep coming back to Body, Food, TV, Sex, Headache, Guilt, etc. You will be stuck in Y (Ego). You are here to cross Y to get to Z.

If you do not cross Y, you will be pulled into X, which will pull you into W. Your job is to move the other way. Cross Y to get to Z and then dive deep into Z.

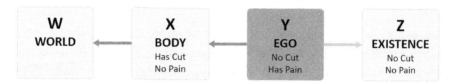

Develop a strong attitude

Therefore be in Surrender with the Guru. Especially when there is pain that is created by a situation with the Guru, the disciple looks to leave, to quit. That is where Surrender has to work, along with Vizhippu Unarvu (Awareness). *Just like a couple that fights sometimes but the wife who decides to stick with the husband despite these fights, in the end will be successful.*

So, from now on have the attitude, that 'I will be in true Surrender with the Guru.' Just like children who naturally Surrender to their parents. Develop the strong attitude that if pleasure comes or pain comes, I will be with the Master so he can have the opportunity to work on me. Sometimes it will be good, sometimes not. That is real Surrender. That will give you the strength to stay strong when Y arises. Otherwise you can't cross Y. You will be pulled to X, the Body level. And that will pull you to W, the World.

SC: So when Pleasure thought arises what exactly should I do?

Mahaprabu: So, remind yourself, from now on you are the property of Mahaprabu, as you have accepted it. Remind yourself there is no such thing as Pleasure, it is just a mental record. Immediately go into Awareness i.e. we are in Y, and need to move to Z. This way you don't give Pleasure a foothold. Our aim is to dive deep into Z. Not stay in Y, or worse go to X or W.

Be on guard, especially with Pleasure. Since with Pain you have a motivation to come out, as no one likes Pain. You'll tell yourself 'There is no such thing as Pain' and try to come out. But with Pleasure you will get caught, and where does it drop you? In Pain!

Surrender keeps you close to the Guru. Then there will be moments when Pain and Pleasure are not there. Only then the Guru works. Other times there are high waves. *How can he send the boat when there is a Tsunami! When there is no Tide, there will be a Ride from the Guru's side, to Abide ... in the Self.*

Effort, Energy, and Experience

I had watched a video of J.Krishnamurthi speaking to someone, where he said (in summary) 'There is nothing you can do. No effort of yours will work.' I have heard similar messages from others too. So I asked Sri Mahaprabu about it. He gave me a strong and convincing response.

That kind of message can be confusing and harmful. Effort alone will take you there. *When the wind is blowing, then only, you are able to feel the presence of the air.* Only when you put in the Effort. Now, how you are able to put in Effort? Because of the presence of some Energy. Prior to any Effort, there will be Energy. Because of the energy alone can you put in Effort. When you put Effort, that will create an Experience about the Energy.

There are three things here: Energy, Effort, Experience. Only the Effort is the bridge between the Energy and Experience. What are you looking for? An Experience. An Experience of what? The Energy. When it can be felt? Whenever you are putting Effort! (Laughing!!).

(SC: Please read the above lines till it is crystal clear what Sri Mahaprabu is saying. The brilliance with which he immediately answered the question with such an apt analogy. The time was past 2 AM! He had already spoken continuously to me for 1 hour and 30 minutes on another topic! This happens every time, no matter what the question is.)

EFFORT $\longrightarrow$ ENERGY $\longrightarrow$ EXPERIENCE

What they mean is that your Effort is only a block when you are in a higher state. There, due to habit, one will continue putting Effort, and that Effort itself will push one back. This is correct for someone who is in a higher state. Until then Effort is a must. If you tell a seeker that Effort is not needed, he will just sit and relax. How will he grow? How will he advance towards the Spirit? How will he move towards the Energy? He is not going to exert. There won't be any exertion. When he puts the Effort, then only there will be a vibration in the Energy. He will hit the Energy. He is going to get the link with the Energy.

SC: And turn its attention, right?

Mahaprabu: Yes, Definitely!

It is simple, remember. Energy and Experience are on two ends. Effort is the bridge. Without the Effort, Energy will be there, but there won't be an Experience of the Energy. The Energy will be there. See, whether you attain Atma Jnana or not. Is Atma affected? Will Atma decrease in intensity if you don't attain Atma Jnana? Or will it increase if you attain?

SC: No, it has no effect.

Mahaprabu: Whether you attain the Experience or not, whether you put Effort or not, Energy will be there. So, what is needed is an Experience of the Energy. You are interested in it. The thirst is born in you already. How do you quench that thirst? Only if you put in the Effort. As you keep on putting Effort and putting Effort, the Experience will be there but as an Expectation. And whenever you are putting Effort, at that moment you are able to feel the presence of Energy. Then, who is putting in the Effort? Your ego may be the one wanting to put in the Effort, a thought. But what comes as Effort, as Thought, as Ego? SC: Energy! Mahaprabu: Yes, what you call Effort, what is its prior form? Energy!! So Energy is the Effort. What you want is the Experience of the Energy. When can you experience it? When the Energy comes as Effort!!

SC: Correct since Energy and Effort are not different, otherwise, there won't be an Experience, since Experience also is Energy!

The 3 are one and the same

Mahaprabu: Correct. All three are one and the same! When you Experience, what are you experiencing? Energy. Is there something other than Energy in the Experience? No. Hidden in Experience is Energy. And what is hidden in Effort is also that Energy. But if it just remained in the state of Energy, then there is no question of Experience at all. The Energy should FLOW! Only for that flowing, an Effort is needed. That's why I said, when air is at a standstill you don't feel it. In summer, people say 'Katthe illa' 'There is no air at all'.

What do they mean? That there is no air? The air is there, but it is still. Just like the energy is always there. Only when it blows he says there is air! For example, *at noon you are in a room. The air is still in the room. It is hot and you are stuffy. You say there is no air at all (If so you'd be dead). But at 12:05 the air blows. You start to feel it. Wasn't the air there at 12:04, 12:03? It was always there, even at 12 but you didn't feel it. Only when it blows, you feel it.* So, in the beginning, to create the Experience, you have to have the air blow. You have to put Effort to get the Experience.

Now, in the same room, even though the breeze is blowing, but say you are in a very bad state of mind. Will you feel the breeze? No. That doesn't mean the air isn't there. So, when it was not blowing, he didn't feel it. When it was blowing also he didn't feel it! So, there is no problem with the existence of the air whether you feel it or not. Thus he will realize that only because it was here in the first place, because it was always here, he was able to feel it later. i.e., Before blowing also it must have been here. Then with maturity, just in the presence of air he will feel it. Because respiration will be happening. There must be air! The one who says 'there is air only when the wind blows', will agree that even without it blowing, there is air. Similarly, by putting in Effort, he who begins to feel the Energy, will one day realize that even without putting Effort, that Energy is there continuously!

I am watching how IT is giving it to you in heaps. (Mahaprabu often reminds us that there is no 'person' talking, or for that matter doing anything. IT speaks. He is referring to the lack of individuality.) Has any university or spiritual book given this equation? Has any spiritual master explained this to you? That too this late at night has any master spoken to you? (It was nearly 3 AM!!). He will say, 'Let's talk tomorrow. What is the hurry!' That is *Arul*, That is Grace, Compassion. Because IT has decided to shower it upon you in abundance. You take one step there. It will take 100 steps here.

Romba Magizchi (Very happy)
Romba Santhosham (Very happy)
Gurudeva
Satguru

With these words, Sri Mahaprabu ended the call.

Where the Ego dies

Sri Mahaprabu was driving to Thiruvannamalai late at night when this conversation happened. It was related to my remark that the Ego is so hard to get rid of. As he does often, Mahaprabu started describing the problem by assigning variables to entities, like building an equation, even instructing me as to how to visualize this.

Take X to be Atma. It is enmeshed in so many records or vasanas over so many births. Call that R. The Ego drives it in this birth. Call it Y. It is the nature of Y to act, resulting in so many Karmas. Call that Z. All actions have results. Call it W. Some actions have positive consequences and some have negative consequences, where positive and negative are just relative. All this is just for your understanding at this stage.

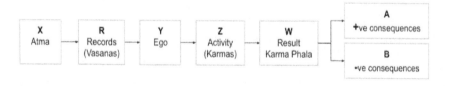

Y, ego cannot stay still. It must act: Z. Actions result in their fruit at some point. The consequences A and B are life. We live in consequences, reacting to them, and performing more actions. That's why Bhagavad Gita says, *Karmanyeva Adhikaraste Ma phaleshu kadachana..* Your right is to effort only. Not the fruit.

Why is the ego Y forced to act? Due to desires. Where do they stem from? From the Records R, the Vasanas. In fact, the Records become Y. The ego Y can't stay still. Its food is activity. Right now for you, Y is being totally controlled by R. You are helpless. That is why the Master is needed. He destroys your vasanas by bringing them up in situations that he creates for you. And as they come, when you are in total surrender, they will drop. As you progress, you start dropping without even asking. *Like if you hold a really hot vessel, you won't even ask 'Should I put it down?'.* If you surrender 100% you can cross A & B and W. This is how it works.

The Ego dies only in Surrender

Then Y will still ask, what to do?

Just the understanding you are gaining when you drop the vasanas each time is enough. Y will still want to know, when will it attain. When it happens it happens.

Remember: Dhyanam (Meditation) etc. are NOT sadhana. They are for your time pass! Because the ego still lives there in those practices. Surrender is the Sadhana. That is the Tapas. The ego dies only there. Constantly remind yourself: I have taken a strong decision to surrender to my Guru. To do whatever he asks me to do, without raising any objections. Stay in that mode.

Surrender is the only way

There is only one way. Only in Surrender will the mind turn off. It is a murder of the mind but like a suicide. Only in Surrender you can keep on putting off the fire of ego as it burns. Look at any Guru. If his disciple had attained Jnana you can be 100% sure that he (the disciple) had surrendered to the Guru. This is why Bhagavan famously said: *'Everyone indeed wants to attain moksha, but when I say "Give yourself unto me" they are unwilling to comply. Then how will moksha be attained?'* These were the words written by Annamalai Swami in his diary. See what a disciple Annamalai Swami was. He totally, unconditionally surrendered to Bhagavan and did whatever Bhagavan asked him to do. For 10 years he mostly did construction work. But what did he come to Bhagavan for? Enlightenment, Sadhana. But see who got Enlightened in the end and who all did not. So many people who consider themselves great devotees of Bhagavan ended up as devotees or pundits and speakers. Why? Because exactly like Bhagavan said. They did not Surrender at the feet of the Master.

The reason is, their minds don't want to surrender their ego. It keeps growing. Mind is like a continuously burning fire. It can burn up more and more with just a small spark, a small wind. Such a thing will not allow you to turn it off. Surrendering to a living Jnani is the only way because he guides you and makes it happen.

Dead Jnani vs. living Jnani

Surrendering to a dead Jnani is like beating a dead snake. You don't need courage. It is meaningless. Surrendering to a living Jnani is like beating a live snake. You need tremendous courage. You need the guts to risk losing yourself.

SC: But isn't there a benefit to praying to Jnanis even if they have left the body?

Mahaprabu: Yes, that prayer is important and is necessary. There is a deep mechanism behind how this works.

As you pray and pray, over time those thoughts get embedded in the Brahma Sakthi that is underlying you. You are sowing the seeds. It is like an auto-suggestion. Prarthanai or Prayer is nothing but sowing the seeds in your own land. Those thoughts will keep sprouting and they turn into actions, results. You will attribute it to God's grace, think it is Bhagavan's grace. Let us look at this closely.

Case 1: Someone who doesn't know anything about Spirituality, God, etc.

Take someone who doesn't know anything, zero about Bhakti, Jnana, etc. But he has a strong value system, a strong willpower that he should live in a righteous way, and deeply wants to live that way. That itself will make it happen. Because he is sowing those thoughts deep down into that same Brahma Sakthi, Iswara Sakthi (Supreme Power). This happens only when someone earnestly wants it. Not just a whim. Yes, the ego is the one that desires to be a certain way, yet who is behind it? The Iswara Sakthi, without which the ego can't function. So what he desires will happen. It might happen now, later or after very long. Depends on the depth of the liking. When it happens, there will be a result, an effect. That effect will be either happiness or sadness. What decides that? The same Iswara Sakthi. And the nature of Iswara Sakthi is one of compassion. So, if the liking is one that doesn't harm him or others, and rather helps him or others, it will result in happiness and it will be long-lasting. Because IT loves all, not just him. Or if the liking is harmful, it will bring sadness. Initially he might be happy, but because it has affected others and they went into sadness, they will all react, since it is the same Iswara Sakti in them. Those reactions will reach him and his happiness won't last. But since he is affected by sadness, after a few attempts he will realize and automatically make an effort to be better.

Over time, this type of person will start to see the pattern and learn to desire things that are good for him and for others. So you see, how by just trial and error the mechanism can make a person like him move toward God. But this trial and error is a very difficult path since he might not have the mental strength to stick with it. He can easily get distracted by happiness or sadness and succumb to destruction.

Case 2: Same as above but he does it with Prayer.

What is Prayer? Is it not a request, a desire for something? It is the exact same mechanism, where you are sowing the seeds. It starts from you alone. Because the Iswara Sakthi is here and now. In you. The difference here is that it is a bit easier since the person praying is putting the burden on God. And as his prayers seem to get answered he will attribute it to God, but when they are not get answered he will still attribute that to God also. In Case 1, when things don't happen, he will try alternate methods. When they fail he could get dejected. And if they succeed he could get arrogant. In prayer, both these risks are mitigated as there will be humility.

So Case 2 and Case 1 are the same mechanism operating behind the scenes. Just that the method is different. Case 2 has a much higher success rate.

Case 3: Surrendering to a dead Jnani.

Say you pray to a dead Jnani and certain prayers are answered. There is a chance that your ego will strengthen. Yes or No? Will the Jnani come down and correct it? Also there is no guarantee that you will always remember every prayer that was answered. You might forget the Jnani's help in the future as your prayers get answered. A dead Jnani cannot question you here or stop you here. It is a one-way street. And when prayers aren't answered, there is a good chance the devotee can get demotivated, even depressed.

Case 4: Surrendering to a living Jnani.

A real Jnani will not let that demotivation happen. He says Yes, you prayed but now you are forgetting it and going off the path thinking that you are responsible for any success or failure. When prayers aren't answered and you feel demotivated, a living Jnani will make you understand the wisdom of the higher power in not answering your prayers. He will remind you that IT knows what is best for you.

SC: Why do people not want to come to living Jnanis? (Having seen many examples of this)

Mahaprabu: They don't want to take risks. They want something safe. They don't want Jnana. They want a safe journey. *It is like a beggar in Tiruvannamalai. He will be sitting there comfortably and relaxed. But compare that to a businessman in the same Girivalam road, especially one starting out new. How active and busy he will be. He won't sit for a minute. Later on, as the business grows and stabilizes, he will become relaxed.* That is maturity. *The beggar on the other hand will want to be very comfortable always. And to help him, there are so many other beggars like him sitting relaxed. He fits right in.* This is what surrendering to a dead Jnani is like.

When you surrender to a living Jnani, after a while he will even discourage prayer. Who is praying? One that doesn't exist. For you to surrender, you should have no agenda at all. So then where is the place for prayer? That's why he asks you to stop.

[Amidst this in-depth conversation, Sri Mahaprabu got a call from his workplace at the college. It is amazing how he talks to them in the same calm way but addresses his seniors as 'Sir' all the time. A great Brahma Jnani addressing his colleagues with respect, without a trace of any pretense or being artificial. He then resumed, exactly at the point he left!]

You see, the lesson changes as you grow. Initially prayer is good for mental strength. You can either come through Bhakti or Self-Trial-and-Error. The mechanism is the same. But eventually, you have to Surrender. And you can only surrender to a living Jnani.

Surrender is a Happening.

It can only Happen. There is no other way. Everything prior to that is just 'Attempts to Surrender'. That's why a living Jnani is important. When you think that you have Surrendered, he will show you that Surrender has not happened. (Laughing). But with a dead Jnani (or a living Ajnani) you will think you have surrendered and keep on going down that path. A Jnani can never cheat you. *He is like a clean mirror. The slightest blemish on your face will be shown back to you clearly exactly like it is.* This is how there is an opportunity for growth in you. Also, he is continuously watching over you. *Like a farmer who watches the land after planting the seeds.*

Obedience, Acceptance then Surrender

Eventually, Surrender will happen one day. That is why before Surrender comes Acceptance. Before Acceptance, Obedience is needed. That is why Guru always stresses the importance of being Obedient, even for the little things he tells you. Obedience is nothing but a fraction of Surrender. Obedience trains your mind to follow the path. If you stay obedient, Acceptance will come. So Obedience is a fraction, a tiny segment of Surrender. Acceptance is a bigger segment. As you grow, it will finally end in Surrender.

Obedience is a decision taken by you. A decision to put an end. If 'you' are putting an end, who do you think started the journey? Only You. See, that also starts with you, aided by Iswara Sakti. Since you started the journey, the journey where you deviated (referring to the original mistake of taking myself to be a separate identity), only you can end it. This is the mechanism. That's why a Master cannot end it for you. You have to work to come out of what you started. See how what I'm saying now (mechanism) aligns perfectly with how we started talking a while ago.

SC: That's why you said a Master is like a pole next to a creeper.

Mahaprabu: Yes, his presence alone is enough.

A living Master will keep on telling you to put an end to the ego, to Surrender. Continuously he will stress that.

But when you try to surrender to a dead Jnani, you will imagine that you have surrendered. You will be confused.

So a living Jnani uses the in-built mechanism to push you out of it. That's why a great saint said:

Thelivu Sri Satguru thiru meni kandal
Thelivu Sri Satguru thiru varthai kettal
Thelivu Sri Satguru thiru naamam cheppal
Thelivu Sri Guru Uru sindhitthal thaane

Just seeing the form of the Satguru brings clarity.
Just hearing the words of the Satguru brings clarity.
Just saying the name of the Satguru brings clarity.
Just remembering the form of the Satguru and thinking about him itself brings clarity.

There is clarity when you see a Guru, listen to a Guru, say his name, or even think of Him. The difference between an *ajnani* and *Jnani* is that one is confused, and the other is clear.

SC: The notion of Doership seems to be the main block for Surrender. That I still have the energy, to put effort to come out of this problem.

Mahaprabu: Very true, Doership is the real problem. If you take it out, surrender will come, and then it is over. To take out Doership you need Obedience, Acceptance and Surrender. So when you practice obedience, remember that the reason you are trying is to remove Doership. That is a mature surrender. Then it will happen fast. That maturity needs to come first. You should understand this and practice Obedience for the right reason. 'I am doing this for my own good.' When you are totally surrendered, it is the end of all *kozappam* – confusion. See, the mechanism is not confused. And whether there is confusion or not, the mechanism is unaffected and stays the same. So it means that the confusion is totally unnecessary, the confusion has no value, yet you are holding on so tightly to this kozappam. And you give it so much value, tremendous value to this life and all your agendas (Laughing.) See what an unfortunate, pitiable state you are in. *Aiyyo*. People are holding onto something that doesn't exist, and they don't want to let it go. Imagine the plight. This is Maya.

Right now the car in front of me has a sticker: *My Grace is Sufficient for you.* See, that Grace is enough to stop the confusion. So, having understood all this, what do we do? Whether you come at it through Trial and Error or Bhakti, till you arrive at the basic mechanism this confusion will be there. So decide. I have started all this (with energy from Iswara Sakthi). I have to end it. No one else can. Guru can only keep on reminding you of this. Why are you suffering. Why don't you stop it? He can't stop it for you. He will not stop asking you to stop!! (laughing). And you cannot do this yourself. Pick a single path: Be Obedient and Surrender. Your end depends on how strong your decision is. Mudivu (the result/end) is dependent on the Mudivu (decision). Mahaprabu pointed out how apt that the Tamil word Mudivu has two meanings: End and Decision.

Mahaprabu is telling all this from experience. He took a strong decision: Without experiencing the Truth I have no interest in life. So let me put an end to this wish, and bring it to fruition. You also can. Do it well. Mahaprabu is with you. Love you. Love you.

Note: Somewhere in this beautiful talk, Sri Mahaprabu told me about how things work with him. He said: When *Cit* sees *Sat*, at those times it will come out as words. If it goes towards *Ananda* then only silence reigns. It will switch off. No words. So the time to capture these words is when *Cit* is talking about *Sat*... Before it goes off into *Ananda*.

Dealing with Lust

In this talk, Sri Mahaprabu spoke about the wrong notions behind lust and told me how to rightly approach it.

Birth itself is because of lust. It is in the genes. Even seeing the inner garment of a woman hanging on a clothesline can kindle it. Then you can imagine! The impression is that happiness comes from the woman's body. As you are more and more in Satsang, as you will constantly hear that happiness is only inside, and slowly as you experience happiness inside, these thoughts will dilute. And once you get the taste of this inner happiness you will not chase other thoughts. You can easily come out of it. Just let it be for now. You have not created it, so don't take responsibility for it. Let it be. Mahaprabu will guide you. The World, Body, Thoughts and Feelings are not me, so Kāma (desire, lust) is also not me. Also, can there be Kāma without Ātma? [At this point a lorry had passed by. It had a message painted on the back, which Sri Mahaprabu not only read to me but took a photo and sent it. It is common to see devotional messages on vehicles in India, but a message like this is very rare.] He said: See how apt the message that just passed in the lorry is: *Aye Maname Summa Iru, Yellam Avan Seyal.* Hey mind, just be still. It is all His work.

It is a wrong impression built over janmās that sexual thoughts are a sin, and therefore it has been covered up. That is what creates guilt. Not the act itself.

It is nature. Accept it. Only then you will come out of it easier. Guilt promotes ego. Don't yield to it. Accept it as good. It is also Ātma.

Surrender it all to the Guru

You need not worry about all this, since you are surrendering with all these. (We had just had a long conversation about Surrendering to the Guru.) It is surrendered to Mahaprabu. It is also a holy thought. Like different flowers at his feet. After surrender, if the thought comes, OK surrender it to the feet of the Master. He has accepted. Let us live with this thought for now, but just become the knower. Not the owner! Observe. You are NOT allowed to become the owner of these thoughts. Based on the maturity of your surrender, instruction will come (have faith and trust). *Clouds of surrender need to be strengthened, then rain will come. When it will come is not up to us.*

We have to treat this problem as follows. *Let us say an engineer is programming a rocket to go into a certain orbit. And it fails. What does he do? He solves the problem in the Rocket, without identifying that I am the Rocket. He does not go to the doctor if his Rocket failed.* (Laughing). Similarly, tell yourself: I am good. The body and mind are not mine. They exist, but they don't belong to me.

You need to rectify a situation but first don't accept that you are the problem. That needs practice. Each Satsang strengthens you. Soon a few words, even silence will hit you. The Spirit will hit you. This needs a strong commitment. At one point hear only one voice inside. That of Mahaprabu. That much attention is needed. That is real tuning. At some point, a resonance will happen. Both spirits will resonate with the same frequency. Only then the real teaching happens. First totally and unconditionally take an oath that whatever Mahaprabu says, I will do. SC must be eliminated. Ātma must be realized. SC cannot eliminate SC. That itself is a real Surrender. Mahaprabu says, if enlightenment is the only goal then there is no way other than Surrender.

Conquering Lust

SC was describing to Mahaprabu how he feels bad about having lusty thoughts at times and used the word 'UnGodly' to describe his feeling of it.

Ungodly?

Mahaprabu: Ungodly etc. is just your mind saying it. Now, since you have defined it as ungodly, let us define what Godliness is, in this context. Actually, let me define it. Did a sperm get created by Godliness or ungodliness?

SC: Godliness.

Mahaprabu: Did the structure of a woman's body and its parts get created by Godliness or ungodliness?

SC: Godliness.

Mahaprabu: Then where did the ungodliness come from?

SC: It came from the mind!

Mahaprabu: Forget about the mind and go one step further. This comes from records i.e. Vasanas. Record A says 'Go for it'. Record B says 'Don't, it is a bad thing'. You have a *shuba vasana* that knows 'Joy isn't there' and an *ashuba vasana* that says 'Lust is joy'. The struggle between these two vasanas goes on and on. And this is just a microcosm of life. All of life is a fight between *vasanas*. The pendulum swings widely between Lust and Guilt. You are going along with it from Left to Right and back again to Left, never centered. Observe it instead and it will stop.

SC: How? I feel like I myself am the pendulum!

Mahaprabu: Actually *penduluma thalravanae needhan. So yeppadi niruthuva.* You are the one pushing the pendulum, so how will you stop it. (Laughing!!) So, when you think that the pendulum should stop, is where you are making the mistake. If you stop pushing it, only then it will stop and stop by its own. *Like a boy who swings on a banyan tree vine, when he lets go and jumps off, the vine still swings for a while due to momentum and soon comes to a complete stop. Just like that, you stop pushing and the pendulum will stop.* This is where honesty is needed from you. i.e. When it stops, do not do things to activate it again, e.g. watching a lusty movie, etc. The pendulum will get confused! It will start moving immediately. Instead, let it go naturally and bring Mahaprabu's memory. You will do it if you are honest. The pendulum will stop. The more you bring Mahaprabu in, the more you will be in the Center.

Conquering Lust

If you can conquer this (lust), i.e. when the oscillation stops and you don't restart it, 95% of your sadhana would be over. All happens with lust as the center. True! Lust is the cause of so many miseries. It is what makes you enter a vagina again. Your desire for a breast puts you right back in the position where you feed from it again. It is this lust that brings you back into rebirth. That is what brings you back again to the earth and binds you to karmas. You keep coming back to earth and each time it is like you are in a maze, lost. If you want to cross the earth once and for all, you have to cross lust. If you do it, 95% of your sadhana is done. All your karmas, sanchita, agami are all designed to take you to the next janma. That is why even in Dhyanam, lustful thoughts will come. The only way out is to transcend it.

As the thought arises, do Japa of Mahaprabu continuously. You will be in the center and the speed of the pendulum will reduce. Even if you have to engage in sex, what the body does there is not important. Your state of mind then is most important. Bring the feeling of Mahaprabu there throughout the act, even during ejaculation. That anandam (joy) is also a gift from the Guru, God. You can't be in Vizippu unarvu (Awareness) then, so bring in the Guru. Even that deed is done in the presence of Mahaprabu. Not thinking of him as form but as the Grace that is always there and does not sleep. That is Mahaprabu. Believe that Mahaprabu is the witness to the act. Bring that strong presence of Mahaprabu as the witness. If you want to realize the Truth, there is no other way.

So, you know that these lustful thoughts are happening. Fine. At that point, bring that feel of Mahaprabu, not as form but as Grace and be honest about bringing that feel there. Only if you are honest this will happen. Otherwise, your mind will tell you 'Let's forget that Mahaprabu for a few minutes, we can always bring him back after the act'. Honesty is key. The honesty should be worthy of the great Uyir, Life that sustains all. That much honesty is needed.

You have to go past it

So, focus on this problem of lust. It has the most energy. Conquer it and you are almost home. I will tell you why it is so difficult. Are you happy when angry? No. Are you happy when you are jealous? No. That is why you drop all those vices. But with Lust, you are happy! That's why you won't leave it. You have strongly recorded in the brain that Lust leads to Happiness. You need to fight it. But you won't fight or cooperate by yourself. Get the Guru's help. If you conquer it, you will see that Kama is nothing but a ray of *Brahmananda* (bliss of the Self). It is the Gate to the temple. You have to go through it. Don't get stuck and keep going back to the gate. Past it is the Temple and Mahaprabu is sitting there as God. He knows. All other vices are easily crossed. This is where you need the most help from Mahaprabu.

SC: Only because of you I am beginning to understand the inner mechanism and that I need help.

Mahaprabu: Yes, so imagine Mahaprabu is there in the room as energy. That is the only way. Don't say 'Ungodliness'. Don't say 'It is all mind created'. Mind is a convenient scapegoat for the ego. Mind has been created just so the ego can say 'I am good, but he is the cause'. Instead, look at what the real issue is. It is because of *Vasanas*. Good. You have started the work. Now you know. No more guilt. Encourage yourself. Don't be discouraged.

Will your mother or father sit with you at 2:30 AM and explain this so clearly to you for 2 hours? Have you helped anyone like this? This is Grace. Without seeing the time or place it gives. You must soak in this Grace. *If you smell a rose, you are near it. You will touch it soon. In other words, if Ātma is a flower, its fragrance is Grace. The closer you are to Grace, you will attain the flower. As you get closer to the flower you will see that only the Fragrance is important. Fragrance is the flower.* Similarly, Grace is God. To realize Grace, become Grace. As you stay more and more with a Guru you will attain Grace since he is Grace.

My Asirvadham (blessing) is that you also should attain the same that I Am. Keep these notes. Let it help the world.

Dealing with depressive mood

In this tremendously insightful talk on sadness, its origin and its cure, Sri Mahaprabu once again helped me understand the problem and taught me the way to come out of it. He went into depth about Atma, the Body, Mind, Vasanas and how they all play a role in sadness.

SC: Once again, I have been going down a loop of thoughts and sadness. Maybe it is due to the absence of things to do, as you have asked me to stop reading as well as many other activities.

Note: Before getting into the details, Sri Mahaprabu cautioned me that what he was about to say was appropriate only for my current level of understanding. It had been less than a year since I had the blessing of meeting Mahaprabu. Later on, more truths will come, he said and then proceeded.

Why we feel sad

Ribhu Gita has a song: *Varruthhamilladhirukkayilum varuthham pola, vazhu utra maa pavi manadhil thondrum.* Actually, there is no *varuttham* (sadness) in you, but still there will be a sadness reflected. You are feeling the effect of it, so there is no denying it. There are a few reasons for this.

First, the ego as it dies slowly, it won't like it. Due to old habits. They are hard to break. For example. *if someone who sleeps a lot during the day starts to break the habit, even if he has decided at the buddhi (intellect) level to stay awake, there will be a longing for sleep.*

Secondly, the *Anma* (Atma) inside is *perarivu* (Supreme Intelligence). As the body gets older and older, whether you accept it or not, Anma Arivu knows this body is getting old. There are two people there. The ego servant who is behaving like a king. And the real king, Atma, who is in sick mode. The original owner is Atma who sees the Servant doing all these things and feels 'I am unable to do anything about it'. The Servant does not care about the body, age, death, etc. Because if not this body, another one will do. *For a thief, if a house he is about to rob is catching fire, he will simply move to the next one. Only the owner of that house will worry about the fire!* So, this is one of the main reasons for depression. Atma will keep showing it to you. Life is expiring. This servant (ego) is destroying you. By the way, for this stage, what I am telling you is correct. As you progress, more truths will come.

All this *Udal* (body), *Manam* (mind), *Atma* are all really a manifestation or an integral part of Ātma only. Body, Mind and Ātma. The Body is like an outer layer of Ātma. Again, just for this state of yours now, what I am saying is correct, so understand it that way. Can there be a body without Ātma? No. That means there is definitely a relationship between Ātma and Body. When the body is affected by disease it will eventually die. Similarly, Mind also develops sickness and is affected. But the body gets affected very quickly. For example, even small things cause immediate allergic reactions. Body is the first victim. For example, when someone cuts you, first the pain is in the body. Next you might feel sad that he did it to you. Where will you find more impact? In the body. Yes, the mind will have some impact but mainly the body. And as you move deeper, compared to body and mind, the impact will be even less on the Ātma. For example, a hand is cut off, still the mind continues. Ātma also continues. All this is for your understanding for now. Hand gone, Mind exists, Ātma exists. Mind has some pain. Ātma is also highly sensitive and intelligent. So it will have some pain. Yet it is surviving, existing. If this is the mechanism, then consider this: One day the whole body will die. But the mind? It will continue. Pain because of the death of the body will be there. Ātma will also have a trace of this pain. That's why the fear of death is there. The mind projects this fear from where? From Ātma. Understand this principle. We are discussing a very important topic. The Body can be destroyed. Mind can be changed and it can forget. For example, it forgets so many injuries, so many deaths. But that trace is accumulated in Ātma for so many births. Can this accumulated cover around it create a happy feeling for Ātma?

Let us say, A is the Body, B is the Mind, C is Ātma, and the cover around it (the record) is R.

This painful trace R is new to this mind (referring to the mind in this life), but Ātma will release it frequently to the mind. For example, *If you keep changing rental homes so many times, you'll forget details about the first home.* Similarly, the mind has forgotten old deaths. It is now only concerned about this body and life. But Ātma has old traces and releases sadness suddenly. Mind B will get confused. 'Everything is going well, why am I sad?' That is why.

SC: But does everyone feel this way?

Mahaprabu: Of course. That's why they watch TV, phones, etc. Only a few like you come to *Anmigam* (the spiritual path).

Understand this well. Just like disease enters a body, the pain will enter from R to Ātma. But Atma can't die. Imagine the *kodumai*, tragedy. R also won't die. It will take energy from Ātma and keep projecting it to the mind. Mind is like a lens. It will keep projecting all these feelings onto you. You will get confused. I've been doing all this to be happy, but I still feel sad and worried. The reason for worry is inside, not outside.

So to overcome this, as you are more and more in Satsang and in contact with the Satguru, he will say: All that is fine. Are you A, are you B, are you R? NO. So try to focus on the freedom of C. Free it from R. But due to habit, we first come to W (World, which is beyond body A) and get stuck there. So many people are stuck in W. There is business, family, education, status, all in W. Beyond W, you will be stuck in Body, then in Mind. Only then you can even touch R. The Master will make you skip all these. Are you W, A, B, R? No. All of these are changing. Why are you bothered about them? The one that is changeless is sick: C. He is like a *maha viran* (a great warrior) who has a boon that he cannot die. But he is tightly bound by an iron *mul veli*, thorn-fence. Will he be free? Happy? No. But he has the boon of immortality. Similarly, we say things like 'Ātma cannot be destroyed, it does not die'. True, but Ātma is also not free! Either he by himself should free himself from the thorn fence. Or someone must help. This is the state of Ātma. If you look at Jesus's photo you will see a *mul veli* around the image of his heart. This is the tragic state. So, if you say I don't know why I'm feeling sad, it is because of this. Can you not accept this scientifically? There is that trace.

Looking to alleviate sadness

You will typically find the solution to sadness where? First in W, World. If World is good, then you will look in A, the Body. If Body is healthy then you'll blame the mind, B. But if Mind is also fine? All are fine. Yet if there is a worry it means there is a reason. Then there is a place where you haven't looked: The record, R. That is where you should look. It is a cover that has to be torn apart. That is the purpose of this life. Life is an opportunity. You can use it for world, body, mind OR you can use it for releasing C from R. So tell yourself, no matter how good the World is, or Body is, or Mind is, still R will keep you dissatisfied. So, take this opportunity to first delete this R. Then, even if World is not good, Body is not good, Mind is not good, You will feel happy. You decide which you want.

This is why no matter what the situation is, an enlightened man is always happy. For example, Bhagavan Ramana Maharishi lived in British India. The country had no freedom, yet he was so happy. But the so-called Mahatma was so sad! Now you can find who was the real Mahatma. Whites were ruling. The country was fearing and doing Namaskara to Whites. But these whites came all the way and were doing Namaskara to Bhagavan!! (Laughing) Indian people were afraid of and fighting for freedom from British people. British people were coming to Bhagavan for their freedom. Write this down and keep reading it when down. (laughing so much). You will get the energy to fight the R.

Be happy. Enjoy. You need Mahaprabu to destroy this R. That is the zone that we need to work. Every second of our life we need to put great effort there. We put so much effort for worldly things, more for bodily things (others can solve world issues but only you can solve your body problem), similarly more responsibility on you to fix any mental issues (at least for body, family can help, but for mental issues very few maybe a friend or book will help). Imagine for R. You have to take complete responsibility.

SC: But we can't see what is in R.

Mahaprabu: But you see the symptom, the effect. With that you come to the Guru. He can see it. You can't do it alone. First you need to understand that you need help. That is called Acceptance or Surrender. People get scared of the word Surrender. Maybe we should call it Acceptance! (Laughing).

We spoke about very important things today. You must put in a lot of effort. Work closely with the Guru and be in contact. Ātma is free, and yet it is bound. Can you honestly say it is not bound? No. That feeling is there. When there is an effect felt, there must be a cause. See at what depth Mahaprabu is speaking from. Also, what I am saying is not just words to you. It is making an impact inside you. It is going inside you. Your entire being is agreeing with me.

As you get to complete acceptance and have a full merging (we are on the way towards complete acceptance now), imagine what it would be like. That is what Samadhi is. It will put you in Samadhi. As you stay more and more in Samadhi, you will get stronger. Right now, you need to go from B to R. But once the merging happens, Guru will push you straight to C. From there you will work on R. There is a big difference.

SC: Did you reach the college Mahaprabu? (I could hear that the drive was over and Sri Mahaprabu was walking inside the college where he works. This discussion started when Mahaprabu was leaving for work. So he described all of the above while driving, signing in at work, walking, etc)

Mahaprabu: Not only that, I'm 4 minutes late. There will be consequences for that. A kind of punishment for that. (SC: Oh!!) Yet HE is talking to you. See, punishment is confirmed, no change in that. Yet he is laughing and talking to you. Because this is what is important. Office, etc. will all go. No one other than Mahaprabu can talk to you like this. I have to be punctual with you more than the office. One of my disciples is in depression. God made me spend the time where it was needed. So, I never bothered about these kinds of problems in the outer world.

Nallapadia nadakattam. May things happen well. *Gurudeva.* (Typically Mahaprabu ends conversations with these words)

Devotion is a must

After Sri Mahaprabu sang a devotional song like he always does with a melting heart, he went into a deep silence. After some time he spoke these words praising the path of Love and Devotion. To attain happiness, we should increase our love for God. Instead, we are all chasing happiness and end up being frustrated.

Is a life where we forget the importance of God even worth living? This should be your attitude: O God, please give me just enough food so I may sing your praise till I die. How can we forget that *Shakti* (power) that produced us? If you want to see God don't see anything else. This situation will come – it already came in my case. (my referring to Sri Mahaprabu).

Instead of fighting with this or that person, taking credit for things, etc. yearn for that situation where all you think of is Him. Can one who asks God for material things ever become his slave? No. You are a slave to that which you ask for. *Bhakti*, devotion, is a must. It must ripen. Mere knowledge is *Kuppa*, garbage. Your ego will make you dance! Think of the *Shakti* that created you and melt. Let it roast you. Every day allocate some time exclusively for God. Ripen, melt in devotion, then you can stand in *Jnana* without ego, without falling. Tell God, I know how dangerous my ego is. I don't want it. I just want to be at your feet. I don't want anything else.

For example, *even to get the friendship of the local village officer how much you have to serve him and his organization. Only then he will even recognize you. Now imagine getting the friendship of the Chief Minister, and then the friendship of a Prime Minister. How difficult.* Now imagine getting the grace of God! How much you have to work to deserve it. Only then can you be really happy. Also, he is ALL, He is Everything. So, try to see him in all; Family, friends, foes, strangers, and finally in the Guru. Obedience, faith and a heart-to-heart relationship with the Guru is what will save you when suffering increases. So, increase those qualities and build a good relationship with your Guru by showing your love and getting his love.

Love, not Knowledge is the Key

You are the *Thuli* (Drop). You have to go to the Ocean (*Kadal*). The Ocean won't come to the Drop. The Drop has to yearn. The Lower has to yearn for the

Higher. It has to be a receiver and stay a receiver. Only then can it attain the higher. Filled with knowledge, how can you receive it? You will only give! Only in melting, *Bhakti, Kalandhu Kariandhu Kanamal Podhal* - mixing, dissolving and disappearing will happen.

What is God's Form?

God's form is Love. For him to come, you have to approach him with Love. If two people approach God, one with Love and the other with Knowledge, TOP PRIORITY will be given to Love by Him. This is my message.

Everyone, by all means, wants only one thing in the end: Happiness. How can it be attained? By Love. If you Love God, Happiness will follow you automatically. But if you love Happiness it will lead to expectation and soon frustration and selfishness. So, Love God.

If you love God, then Happiness will follow you automatically

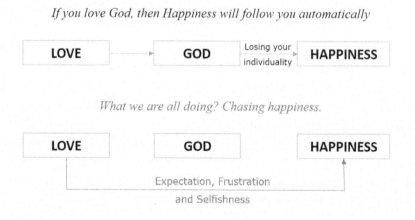

What we are all doing? Chasing happiness.

Directly you cannot go to Happiness, but that is what we are ALL trying to do. So give your total love to God, the Supreme Power, the Guru. To nothing else. Then your selfishness will go. And what comes as a result? Happiness. Since losing your individuality leads to Happiness. The love you show God/Guru, He multiplies it N fold and returns it to you as Happiness!

God refers to that nameless, formless, indestructible, eternal Existence which is filled with Love and Intelligence, which is appearing here as everyone and everything.

Thinking makes me mad

Lately I had been going back and forth between Bhakti and Jnana, Devotion and Self-Awareness. It got to a point where I could practice neither. I was blessed to have the opportunity to share my struggles with a *Jnani* Sri Mahaprabu. Not only did he set things right, but the conversation was also so jovial. He showed me that all these problems are not for Atma. They are for the ego, and (sadly) it is this maddening effect of thought that ultimately leads one to drop thinking itself. 'You are on the right track,' he said!

SC: At times I become a victim to my mind and even feel like I'm going mad.

Mahaprabu: Atma doesn't care if you attain it or not. So who needs it?

The Unreal (imaginary idea of a person) wants to attain the Truth. Look at this carefully. The Unreal itself is the *Sikkal*, the real problem. But our focus is not on the Unreal. Our focus is always on the problem, the suffering! In other words, we want to make the Unreal have no problems, have no suffering! Your unreal still has the energy and thinks it has the ability to solve its problems. The solution is to shift out of the Unreal. You can't do that by yourself, which is the same Unreal. But still you have hope that with effort someday you can. Which shows you still have capacity. But the goal is to shift to effortlessness. For this, total trust in the Master is what you need. Not answers to questions on how to solve your problems.

You said you feel like going mad. Drop that feeling. Lose the capacity to hold on to it. Holding is energy. That needs to be dropped. But you can't do it. Since you are used to bad habits of concepts, ideas etc. which you have accumulated through reading and thinking. Only when you become totally tired of thinking you will not think further about stopping thinking.

How to come out of this

Summa Iru. As Bhagavan said, 'Just be'. But only after exhaustion this will happen. As you travel with Guru it will start to happen. For example, it is like this: *You are going at a high speed in your car due to the energy, but it is going in the wrong direction. But you think you are going home. In reality your home has already passed. But you won't realize that even if told. So the Guru comes alongside in his car and befriends you. Slowly he overtakes you and goes in front of you. Then he starts to slow down for a while without alerting you to the fact that you are also slowing down. Then he comes back alongside to journey with you.* (We were both laughing so much as Mahaprabu was describing this. And with most of his anecdotes, the written word does no justice. Listening to him live and sharing that divine laughter of his is an experience in itself.) *In this manner, he slowly brings you to your home, even though you don't realize it is your home. Once both cars are inside the compound, he quickly closes the gate! The funny part is that you still don't think that's your home i.e. You haven't realized your true nature yet. So even in the house, just for your sake, the Guru draws roads so you can slowly keep driving!!!* (The way Mahaprabu was depicting all this with his humorous words, my stomach could not take the laughter anymore! All my frustrations at the beginning of the call had vanished unknown to me.)

So, your thinking capacity has to go 100%. *Even a single root of a plant that is left behind after the plant is cut, can grow back into a tree.* Right now, everyone needs *Anbu* (Love) and *Bhakti* (Devotion) on the *Perarul* (Supreme Grace). We need to shift from mind to heart. From Car to the House. Just follow what I say. When I say drop, you must drop without question. Only up to a point the Guru can use words. As you progress, he can't use words after some point.

Now we are shifting from thinking to being. You'll drop thinking only when thinking burns you like fire. That's why I said we are in the right direction when you said it feels like you are going mad.

There is a Supreme Intelligence. (*Perarivu*). The body is proof of it. How ingeniously complex and capable it is. Bow to that *Perarivu*, Supreme Intelligence. *Panivu* (obedience, humility) will come. Obedience must be 24 hours. That is the zone I'm expecting for you now for 24 hrs. Do you have that firm feeling inside you? Our goal is *Perarivu*. Is our attention on it? *Andha ninaivu*, that continued remembrance is called Devotion. It is needed now. Only when you understand that knowledge won't help, will you drop it.

IT is doing an amazing job continuously. Keep feeling that. Your ego will reduce. No more thinking. We are moving correctly. Everything should be that Supreme Intelligence for you. Devotion to it is needed. And don't bother about *Dvaita* – duality (Since SC had remarked earlier, his difficulty with prayer sometimes as it still is steeped in duality). Only those who bother about *Dvaita* will be debating it, discussing it. Because if you bother about whether you are in *Dvaita* or *Advaita* (non-duality) then definitely you are in *Dvaita*!!! Devotion to that Supreme Intelligence will appear as *Dvaita* now, but one day you will disappear.

Note: At the end of this conversation there was no trace of any suffering or worry in me. Not only was I blessed with the right understanding of what was happening to me, he also showed me once again that I cannot think my way out of this mess created by the I. Simply staying in Surrender to the Guru, and following his words is enough. That's all.

Importance of Grace

Sri Mahaprabu points out that even after we develop a proper understanding that joy and sorrow are creations of the mind and have no basis in reality, when situations come, this understanding will not come to our remembrance. Remembrance comes by Grace alone. But one has to keep trying and work really hard to deserve Grace. And finally, when the futility of effort is realized, a Surrender happens. Grace comes through this Surrender in the form of the Guru.

If you cooked for 100 people, different taste buds will react differently and that's fine. Nothing more. Their feedback will be based on that. Some will praise your cooking, others will complain. Or some of them may hate you and purposely say it was bad. Either way, all are opinions only. Plus 'you' did not really cook the food. But see how each opinion impacts you. When praised you feel good. When criticized you get upset. But since the 'you' that cooked the food is itself an illusion, the Happiness and Sorrow that come from their praising or criticizing the food are also mere opinions based on that illusion. It has nothing to do with reality. Unbelievably Stupid!

So leave all opinions behind, and live based on fact alone. Existence, or Energy as a nameless, formless Being is Existing here and now without the help of anyone to know it is here, and IT helps you know you are here and now; that Existence is NOT AN OPINION. It is a fact. So it is common to ALL. That I am an individual, male, father, husband are all OPINIONS only. From these come your happiness and sorrows, which are also opinions. They seem real but are entirely ILLUSIONS, like a mirage. YOU ARE ALSO AN ILLUSION. Understanding this ignorance and getting rid of this ignorance is called Self-Realization.

So, first you must change your entire lifestyle. Right now you have a clear understanding that happiness and sorrow, pleasure and pain are all opinions, illusions, not facts. This understanding in you should lead to a thirst to remove this ignorance. This understanding must become a habit and this understanding must come to your remembrance when you slip. But 'you' cannot bring it to your remembrance when you slip. It needs the blessing of God, Guru, elders, parents, well-wishers etc. But above all when you are blessed by an enlightened Master it will nullify everything and give you the boost. That is why it is said: *Guru Brahma, Guru Vishnu, Guru Devo, Maheshwaraha. Guru Sakshat Param Brahmam, Tasmai Sri Gurave namaha.* And the great saint, Thiru Moolar has said: *Seeing a Master, Hearing his words, Repeating a Master's name – or at least remembering him in your heart: All will give you that clarity.* If you have sincere devotion and do dedicated service to your Guru., then that understanding will come at the right moment and protect you. Even now, see how many times you forget this in day-to-day activities. Therefore, more devotion and more service is needed to get more *Arul* (Grace). Keep on begging in prayer for that *Arul. Ayya Arul thaa* - O Lord, Please shower your Grace on me. *Kelungal Kodukka Padum,* Ask and it shall be given, said Jesus. You must ask. Only that *Arul,* grace carries forward from birth to birth.

Grace has to be earned

Grace is there, but you have to earn it. *It is like a person who is in jail for a life sentence. He wants a pardon, and the pardon option is there. But he has to work tremendously hard for it in prison. Only then there is even a chance that he is eligible for it.* For Mahaprabu also, he could not remember it by effort. It was Grace alone. But until that point, only God knows how many *janmas* (lives) of all kinds of effort he has put in. You have to keep trying to remember, keep on trying, and one fine day when you have given up, then *Arul* comes in the form of the Guru, coming down to work for you, to help you get the Grace. Then you have surrendered. Everything before that is an effort by the Ego. That effort is always short-lived since the ego has expectations, which always ends in frustration. As a result, you will give up. Only after you surrender, the real work starts. All efforts before that are preparation.

The ego wants to be without ego! This is an ego-effort. But one day that ego also will drop. That will only come with Grace.

Grace requires Surrender

To ask for Grace you cannot have ego. The great master Yogi Ram Surat Kumar came to Tiruvannamalai after enlightenment and yet begged for his food. In Sri Bhagavan's Arunachala Siva song, he begs Arunachala: *I am just a piece of iron, you are the magnet!* Imagine. This is Bhagavan Ramana Maharshi singing to the Supreme Power. To get Grace, Surrender is the only way. Then when pleasure and pain come, you will remember that they are illusions. Especially when pleasure comes it is very difficult to remember, since you are enjoying and will easily forget. Blessing is needed. For that blessing, be prepared to do anything. Even give your life. I have got that blessing so many times. Bhagavan, Osho and specially Avudai Akkal have all blessed me.

Grace comes through the Guru

All Jnanis' Grace comes through your Guru only. It is like this: *A Tahsildhar (a worker relatively low in the ranks) wants his salary. The District Collector has to sign the papers and only then it will be released, but it is not happening for some reason. Even if the Tahsildar goes to the Chief Minister, the Chief Minister will simply say 'Go to the District Collector'.* Same thing here. The Seeker is the Tahsildar. The Supreme Power is the Chief Minister. Guru is the District Collector! The thing is, even the District Collector knows that it is not his personal money, yet only if he signs, the money will be released. Mahaprabu is like that District Collector. This is to emphasize how through the Guru alone, the blessings of all *Brahma Jnanis* will come. That is why I invoke "*Anaithu Brahma Jnaanigalin Arul Undagattum.* May all the Brahma Jnanis shower their blessings." (Note: Every single Satsang with Mahaprabu ends with those words of blessings from him.) So love and serve with total dedication. This earth is a temporary tourist place. Use everything, but with the right approach that nothing is mine. Since you don't own anything really. You came empty into this world and will go empty.

Then Sri Mahaprabu urged us with these words:

It is a free-flowing system, a Happening. 'I' and 'Mine' were the obstacles to the flow. 'I' am Gone. Now I am free with the flow. I am giving my best due to love and gratitude. Kindly accept it with Surrender.

Suffering and its Solution

I was feeling terribly down the last few days. Despite Sri Mahaprabu's continuous reminders to stay focused on our purpose, I had willfully gotten myself into a project. It sucked up all the time and the mind totally embraced the distraction since it didn't have to sit down and meditate, pray, etc. As a result, I stopped doing my daily *dhyanam* (meditation) routine. Instead, I was consumed by this project. Soon enough the guilt and worry overtook me. I felt miserable, which in turn prevented me from getting back. Also, I had not spoken to Sri Mahaprabu one-on-one in some time. This aggravated things further.

That morning, Sri Mahaprabu called while driving back to Chennai from Tiruvannamalai.

A lot of good things are happening (I am guessing he is referring to the continuous Satsangs for 50+ days during the Covid lockdown). *Ulagathuku vandhadhurkaana kaaranangal nadaipetturikku.* The purpose for which we came to this earth is being fulfilled. (Referring to the attempt to know the Truth about ourselves.) People keep coming back to the earth millions of times and getting caught, again and again. Imagine going to Kutralam Falls millions of times. The Earth, Bhoomi is a grain of sand in the universe. It is limited. Our infinite nature is limitless. That is our originality. But we have become trapped and keep coming back to this earth again and again, starting from scratch. Even if you come just once, you should be happy. Treat it like a fun, tourist place. Instead, we get caught indf suffering. Ignorance is the cause.

(On hearing this I decided to bring up the mental agony I was going through. After sharing it, I said 'I am observing myself go down. I can see it.')

Beautiful explanation of Suffering

Don't observe. Pray. You said it is unbearable. Then why are you sitting there simply observing it? Does watching it make it better? No. A deep prayer is needed. All kinds of weapons must be used to fight the enemy. *You see Gods, with 12 hands, each hand with a different kind of weapon!* Nallapadiya Nadakkum (all will be well.) It is just a block. 25 years back you wouldn't have

85

known this block. I have told you, anytime you need to speak to me, call immediately. Only by talking to me, will certain things clear up.

SC: I feel that all these problems are really self-created. For example, I feel bad that I have an ego and suffer that I am like this!

Mahaprabu (laughing): See how strong, how tricky that ignorance is. Don't analyze it. Surrender, Surrender. Tell yourself. "I will only listen to Mahaprabu. OK ego, you do whatever you want. I have Mahaprabu. He has told me: 'Whoever has a deep-rooted ego, that's where he likes to focus!'" Tell it that.

Let's look at it. Actually, the ego you mention, does not even exist. It is just a bad dream. Whether it is bad or really, really bad, does not matter. It is a dream. To put it another way, *whether you earn 10 Rs or 10 Lakh Rs or 10 Crore Rs in a dream, all are the same. They have Zero value when you wake up. (Laughing) Once you wake up from the dream you cannot do anything with that money. Nothing.* Similarly, the only value you need to give your ego and suffering is Zero. You will be free one day. The ego is like a dream. It is imagination.

Thookathil Karpanai = Kanavu [In sleep when you imagine it is called a Dream]

Viziippil Karpanai = Ahandhai [In waking state when you imagine it is called Ego]

SC: So, the opinion of myself that I have all these Kama, Krodha, Loba, Moha etc. is all an Imagination?? (Desire, Anger, Greed, Delusion, etc)

Mahaprabu: Of course!! All a dream! But this suffering in the waking state has a slight advantage over suffering in a dream. Because in your dream at night I cannot come and tell you it is a dream.

SC: Wow! All an imagination. Even though I know it in theory, when you say it, it hits me.

First step *liye nee vazukki vizundhutta.* You have slipped and fallen down in the very first step and rolled down 50 steps. Then there is a landing. Then from there you have fallen another 20 steps. *Urundu vandhutta.* You rolled down those 20 steps. Now you are telling me you fell 20 steps. I am seeing that you have fallen 70 steps! since 20 is just from the landing. Because you have already lost Awareness. *Thani Nabar* (individuality) is not something that exists. If it really existed, then I can understand. For e.g. if you have a wound on your body from an injury, and if I say "that injury is not real" you can object. But ahankaram (ego or individuality) is an *illadha onnu* (non-existent thing). It does not exist. But you have accepted it for a long time and lived with it. So then, what should be your Saadhana? *Nabar thanmayin adipadaiyil seyalpaduvadhai muzuvadhumaaga vittu pazagudhal.* (Mahaprabu is reminding me of Step 1 of his 3-step process.) *Practicing living without acting on the basis of a person.*

Call this personhood or ego (*Nabar Thanmai*) as X.

Call Y, this *'Ayyo, nabar thanmai vandhudche'* (Oh! my mind/ego is messing me up again), and the resulting suffering.

Call Z, *'Andha suffering vandhudche ennu suffer pandora'*, Oh! Worrying and suffering that the suffering has started (Laughing).

See you are suffering because of Z right now. (Laughing). Z came from Y. Not from X. See, Y and Z become a bundle. Both are suffering. See how bad X is. Now I ask you to put all the sufferings into a bag labeled 'Suffering'. Which would you put? You would only put Y and Z, but who is the culprit? X. You should throw him also in the bag!!! (Laughing). X is the first generation that gave birth to Y, which then gave birth to Z. So, if Y and Z are suffering, its parent that gave birth, that produced it is also Suffering. Therefore X (Ego, *Nabar Thanmai*, Individuality) is Suffering too. You are feeling and fretting about Y (Suffering) which gave birth to Z. But which should you have felt about the most? X. But you left it out. That is where Awareness, *Vizippu Unarvu* is needed. You worried about Y and gave birth to Z. So much attention you gave to Y and Z, why didn't you give it to X?

SC: Because I am tightly identified with X so I didn't see it as a separate troublemaker.

Mahaprabu: That's it!

How to come out of Suffering

That's why to break that, to make that separation, the only way is to work closely with the Guru while being in total Surrender. It (suffering) won't let you go. Even I cannot separate it suddenly from you. I can't hit it. Why? You have protected it with comfort and in a sophisticated way, like a spoilt child. Mahaprabu can't put too much pressure. You won't be able to tolerate it. I need to take you out little by little. Even though your mind wants a quick solution, your heart has to cooperate. The inner system has to cooperate and that is what is happening. See, you yourself said it, 'I am so tightly identified with it.' Because you 'are' it in your mind. *It is hard to untie a knot that is so tightly bound. Slowly we have to shake it, push it, pull it, adjust it.* Same way here also. But we don't need to worry about it. Doesn't matter how tight it is. The fact remains that 'I am a person' is just a thought. Even if it was tight, it is still a thought. So, keep that in mind. It may be tight, no problem! It is only a thought. Just a matter of time. Accept the fact that it needs to be given time. You can't want the knot to be removed fast.

SC: Thinking that I want it out fast is itself strengthening it.

Mahaprabu: Exactly. Understand this very carefully. You are not stuck somewhere and need to free yourself from it. You are already free. You are behind it all. In front of you there may be a lot of drama. (Laughing). Always go to the back and stay (referring to feeling my Existence, which is the substratum of everything). You are there separate from it all. Don't forget. Staying without forgetting is *Jnānam*, Enlightenment.

When the knot feels tight, at those times you need to work to loosen it. That means giving it full attention, reminding myself that I am not a separate person, so why go and get stuck in all this. That is where you must work. That is the right time to work. Have your *satsang* then! Even being aware that you feel the knot being tight and heavy, is great. Thank Grace for that Awareness. Then if you feel strong you can work on loosening it through Awareness. If you don't feel strong then pray. Pray to the Guru at that point, that the next time it comes please give me the energy to loosen it. Only if you ask you will get it. IT wants to give even if you don't ask. So, if you ask, won't it give? That's its nature. Ask it. Demand it. You have the right. We are the reflection of God. A fraction. We are part and parcel of Godliness. We are not a part and parcel of Ugliness. Value that. It is real.

This is the work. This is exactly where you need to work. This is the inner work. You need to excel here. As soon as you identify a knot, get ready. It's time to work. Don't divert it with TV, food, etc. (Wow! how does he know!) This is the right time. This is your turn. Sit then for meditation. If you have the strength you can work. If not Pray.

SC: That is when I become a victim.

Mahaprabu: This is the insight you needed. Mahaprabu is with you. Do it beautifully. Take notes. Recall, digest, analyze. Make yourself understand at a deep level. Only then it will come when needed. Only if you have *bhakti* and *shraddai*, devotion and sincerity, it will stay at the right level and surface when needed. Only he who has Guru bhakti and is in total surrender, only for him this *upadesam* (teaching) will work. The seed may be great, but the land needs to be fertile. For your part you need to have *Bhakti* and *Shraddhai*. That

88

is making the land fertile. In normal times, immerse yourself in *Bhakti*, *Shraddha*, whatever works for you. Grow those fast. It like driving on a highway. When there are no blocks, no traffic you should drive fast. When there is a block you can't go fast, so you'll need to work extra. We forget this when things are going well and waste our time. So, whenever you have the strength, work. If not Pray. This strength can be developed only when things are going well.

The good thing is now that you now know all this. The light is there. You should appreciate that. It may not be bright, but you have a ray of understanding. That is enough for now. All these days you didn't have it. Now trace the ray. Even if the ray disappears, don't worry about the darkness. Just remember, there is a ray. (Laughing). That's all you need. We have seen it. It exists. And you've seen that when the ray comes, the darkness goes. They can't coexist. Light is more powerful than darkness. So, which has a permanent existence? Light. Celebrate it. Darkness is temporary. Even in darkness you can celebrate.

SC: Because to know that you are in darkness itself is a ray of light. So celebrate. Is that what you mean?

Mahaprabu: Exactly. What more do you need! Call me anytime you need. I am there for you. Just pick up the phone and talk. Only then you will get it. Wonderful. Just remember. *Nee Illai.* You don't exist. How much you believed that you (as an individual) existed. Did you have any doubt? With that same intensity, be absolutely sure that you don't exist. Something else is there. *Once you know that you have been occupying someone else's house for so long and now you find out, won't you feel ashamed?* (Laughing). Feel that shame strongly. This is a long process. It all comes down to your honesty. Mahaprabu insists that you must let it go, drop it. No other way. There is no compromise. Stay alert. Be in *Satsang*. You have to keep working continuously. A lot of work needs to be done. If you drop the work it will strangle your neck.

How are you?

This is a question that Mahaprabu never asks. But today he did. It was 2 months since he came to Tiruvannamalai due to the strict lockdown on travel due to the Covid situation. (Daily Satsang has been going on through WhatsApp without a single day missed). But this is the first instance in 15 years that he has missed coming to Tiruvannamalai on a weekend. The lockdown still is in place but Sri Mahaprabu rode a bike up to a mid-way point, changed bikes, and arrived at the Rest House. He took a few minutes to freshen up and gave the following talk explaining what he meant by that question: How are you.

Who does that question refer to? It can be 3 things. Ātma which is existing here and now is always fine. So, the question is not regarding Ātma. Next, the Body. The body is always not fine. It keeps changing. 1 hour back you might have had some pain, but not now. Even routine tasks such as passing motions/toilet habit is different from day to day. Due to the usage of the body, there will be deterioration over time, so really the question does not refer to the body either. Next: Thoughts. About Thoughts alone, you can ask. Only thoughts can be good or bad.

When Mahaprabu asks "How Are You", it means are your thoughts good. Are they helping you to go towards the Source? The group of thoughts that help you move inward and abide in the source, those are good thoughts. So many thoughts are going on, so when I ask you "How are you?", it means how are your thoughts. *Thoughts are like clouds. Even though we are the sky, at least let us be like white clouds because the Sun penetrates through them easily. If you go to the Sun, then you can go to Sky. The Sun = I Am ness. White clouds = Good Thoughts. Dark clouds create fear. They are the thoughts that have been creating fear from young.*

I hope that all of you are well. I assume that you are all well.

The one thought that matters

Only one thought matters. If you think that you are the Ātma, a deathless being, beyond body, beyond mind. It may be a thought but it will change the total scenario. On the other hand, if you think you are the body, the whole picture is different.

It is like a toggle key. Who is having this choice? It is in your hands. Not in others' hands. If you think you are the deathless being, then no more thoughts, silence, a feeling of peace and security, a complete detachment immediately from all miseries. If you are able to disconnect immediately and dive into tremendous peace it is a good sign. That you are in a good state. It shows an improvement. The moment you think you are a deathless being, you can disconnect.

How to do this? Consciously avoid thinking that you are an individual. Various situations present themselves continuously. Ātma or Source or Self is not somewhere else. You are it. It is You. In a split second, you can lose yourself. So consciously in various situations, you must be alert in NOT thinking that you are the body. And voluntarily you should expose yourself to various situations such as Low, Medium, and High based on your ability so that you can experiment with this. Voluntarily and honestly you should do it. When you find that you are able to abide in the Self in all 3 situations, then you will have confidence in yourself, which will push you upwards.

All is in your hand. You have given your heart to me, but everything else is still with you. Why do I ask for your heart? Because unknowingly you should not give it to others! *I'm like the locker in the bank. All your hearts are deposited with me.* As your heart is with me I am able to connect with you all. And as we are able to establish this connection, my words will go inside you and they will work. They will work because these words are coming from my heart. My heart is always towards you all. But if your heart is in some others' hands they will put a gate around it and then my words won't work. When your heart is with me it is like your address is Care of (%) Sri Mahaprabu. But if it is with someone it is % Someone. Your address might be "care of someone" but they will not take care of you!

So where must your effort be?

On Thoughts. There are only 2 options for thoughts. Either the thought that you are the deathless being, Ātma, or the thought that you are an individual. If you are not sticking to the thought that you are a deathless being, if you are not doing things carefully with awareness, then you are not holding on to the thought of you as a deathless being. So then, automatically you will hold on to the thought that you are an individual. Both are thoughts, but which one you hold on to makes all the difference. You must practice this very honestly, consciously. The thinking process or ignorance can be killed only by the honesty of your practice. That alone can kill your ego. If the Master could kill the ego directly, one Buddha would have been enough. It does not work that way. So, he is doing the killing by asking you to be honest in your practice. He is establishing the mechanism inside you to kill the ego. Once it is established, whenever the ego comes, the mechanism will cut it. It is called Self-Killing. A single master cannot cut the ego of so many disciples, especially since the ego is continuously rising at different times even in one individual. So, develop honesty. Do the practice in 3 categories of situations, Low, Medium, and High risk. Once the ego is completely killed and you have tasted the joy of the deathless existence, living as the deathless one, once you have tasted that, enjoyed that, then the mind has that ability to be there automatically. For example, *once a person has tasted alcohol and enjoyed it, there are more chances for him to get it again and again. He will seek that. Even so, due to ethics and health concerns, he might avoid it. But if a person indulges once in a sexual relationship, will he say "Hereafter I won't indulge in sex". Again and again he will want to.* Why? It is the nature of the mind. It notes that some happiness is coming out of that act. Again and again it will ask. It will follow that track. By using this nature of the mind, once you make it taste the inner presence, it will ask for it again and again. If it is not happening, if it is not asking, that means you have not tasted it. That is the scale. Is it not true? A simple fact.

The whole effort is to enjoy it once

The whole effort is to get the brain to enjoy the taste for the first time. For this, we are struggling. It is a struggle because the mind says: I found happiness here and there. But the Master keeps saying: Happiness is not anywhere. It is inside. This is the struggle. Once you understand the struggle you have crossed half the way. As you don't know that it is a struggle, you do it like a part-time job. Why part-time? Because the mind is continuously saying "if you do this you will be happy; if you do that you will be happy." And as for going inward to seek happiness? That is just a hope. You have not experienced it. You have heard all saints say it, so you know something must be there. Based on that tiny hope you are putting in effort. So it won't have the natural potential, since you don't have the experience. You entered this realm through the study of Scriptures, various Satsangs, the pull of the Master, etc. It is a pull. Rarely do sorrows push you into spirituality. The majority of the time, your mind is working towards where it thinks happiness is. It has its own compartments for sources of happiness. Compartment A, B, C, D, etc. Even chatting unnecessarily is a compartment. So, the mind will keep working in compartments A, B, C, etc. In one small compartment is Spiritual Enlightenment! That's why it is a part-time job. That is why you cannot give it all of your natural strength. The mind won't cooperate. It will drag you to other compartments. Only by constant Satsang and when you put the effort in the right place continuously, you will progress and develop confidence. That will extract the natural potential within you. This will push you up and you will enjoy the presence inside. Once you have tasted it, then the mind will cooperate. Before that, it might be an obsession. But once it tastes, it will be a progression. Then it will say, "What is there in A, B, C!" The same mind will drag you to Spiritual Enlightenment. It will only want to go inside. Finally, the whole thinking process will dissolve. According to the situation, the system will look all around and make a decision and move on to the next moment.

Meditation is not a Practice

An eye-opening talk on the fundamentals of Meditation by Sri Mahaprabu, where he points out what it is NOT and the difference between doing vs. happening. And what really is in our hands when it comes to Meditation.

Meditation is a 24-hour phenomenon, a natural one. One cannot practice it. So if you try to practice meditation it will be a failure. When you sit for meditation, the mind that says 'I should meditate properly' is a disturbance. Disturbance to what? The Silence... which is the state of Meditation! And when you are not meditating, after some point the mind will start nagging. 'You need to meditate. You are not meditating enough..' This is also a disturbance to the Silence. It is also caused by the same mind. Accepting the mind's demand to meditate (in both situations) is like giving half of the dark room, the name 'Light'. It is the mind that is creating a feeling called 'I am meditating'.

If you see a signboard that says 'Sleeping taught here' wouldn't you laugh? Similarly, if you see a place that says 'Meditation taught here' it should elicit the same laugh. Both are the same.

Meditation is not a practice. But people keep on practicing. Meditation is not an activity. Meditation is Rest, like sleeping. Sleeping is nothing but a rest. If you drop all other things, let's say the 'rest' of the things, you will come to rest! Meditation is a 24-hour phenomenon, a natural one. One cannot practice it. So if you try to practice meditation it will be a failure. Because you are doing something. Consciously you start doing something. When you do something unconsciously it won't trouble you. But whatever you do consciously is the problem. 'I have done this, so I expect these things to happen'. Even during Meditation, consciously you are doing it. Therefore you are expecting something to happen. But it will not happen. Because 'you' are very much there. If you persist with this effort you could even become a psycho-patient.

Fundamentals of Meditation

We have to understand the fundamentals of meditation. Meditation is not an activity. It cannot be done. Then why do people, even spiritual Masters ask disciples to do Meditation? Mahaprabu also asks, have you done meditation?

To make you understand that at some point when you keep on trying to meditate, at some point you yourself will know that it cannot be done. When you consciously understand that it cannot be done, what will you do? You will stop it. When you stop it, you are in Meditation. This is a kind of mad game. No other way. In all other activities if you start doing them, they will multiply and go on. But meditation if you do it as an activity it will not multiply, it will not give any reply!

Even if you understand through my words, if you are able to accept my words that Meditation is not an activity and it cannot be done, your mind will not listen to it. Again it will go on trying Meditation. Because in all other things, consciously you are doing. The mind is doing. Automatically in this also the same habit will come. You will forget my words that Meditation is not an activity, it cannot be done. Automatically your mind will engage you in meditation. Unconsciously it is engaging you. But you will reach a point where consciously you will understand that it just cannot be done. Since you consciously understand, at that point you will not do anything. That conscious non-doing is called Meditation.

Then since through your experience you are able to understand when Meditation is happening, under what circumstances it is happening; when you are able to understand all these things consciously, then you will allow or create an inner and outer atmosphere so that those non-doing moments will occur again and again. You will create an ambiance for that, as you have the knowledge and experience of what Meditation is. From there you are growing. Then that space, the duration will expand. You will be very happy. It will be astonishing. You will be astonished that we have not done anything but something is happening!

Doing vs. Happening

For the first time, you will understand the difference between doing and happening. Then by having a clear understanding of the difference between these two, whatever needs to happen you will allow it; whatever needs to be done you will do it. Happening is not in our hands. Doing is in our hands. Since we don't have this understanding, we are trying for the happening and we are not trying for the doing. We are creating a very big complexity for ourselves. Then we say life is so complex!

But life is really very simple. This understanding is needed. This understanding happens only by experience. To get the right sense we have to pass through so many nonsenses. Nonsense is just the previous stage in the course of evolution to get to sense. So, all complexities are happening because of this first complexity. As we don't know the difference between doing and happening, we are trying to do whatever is happening. We are not trying to do whatever can be done. We are wasting energy, material, etc. Finally, frustration is the result. So those who experience tremendous frustration, that is the first criterion to attain enlightenment! So whenever you are frustrated in your mind, you think of that as a blessing. Just like you move from nonsense to sense you will move from Frustration to Celebration.

It is like sleeping. When we create the right atmosphere for sleep to happen, then automatically sleep will come. Like this, if you create the right atmosphere, both inner and outer, then meditation will happen. As your mind is steeped in stupidity and nonsense it will not allow you to create the right atmosphere. It will create a good atmosphere for 'its' survival, for the survival of ignorance. Based on ignorance whatever situation you create is not going to give you light. When someone is in darkness, when they have NO idea about light; when they only know darkness and they are living in darkness; there how can they think about light? Somebody in a darkroom says I am going to find light. Yes, he will find light, but that will just be another kind of darkness. His mind will give it a name called light. In the darkroom, to the left it is dark, to my right it is light! So, those in ignorance cannot think about intelligence by themselves. Intelligence is also a happening. It will happen, that's all. The sun has to come. Then you will see, oh, this is light. Only at that time can you know the difference between light and darkness. Similarly, when intelligence comes, darkness will go. Then you will have the experience of these two phenomena. You will keep yourself in the natural system. Then, when ignorance comes you will be alert. When intelligence comes you will be happy and celebrate. *When the sun is up, the mother allows the children to play happily. When it becomes dark she brings them inside to protect them.* Then one day you will go beyond these two and be the witness.

Creating the right atmosphere for Meditation

SC: But I cannot create the conditions/atmosphere for meditation, because if I did so it would be my mind doing it!

Mahaprabu: Yes, you cannot. Since you cannot do it, you have to depend on the Master. Depending on the Master is Surrender. As we move from ignorance to intelligence we have to go from dependence to independence. If you are in Surrender, then the Master is able to create the right situation for it to happen. You cannot create it. For sleep, you know very well, so you can create the right atmosphere. The one who knows about it alone can create it. So, the Master creates the right atmosphere in which you can experience Meditation that is happening. But for that, your knowledge, your intelligence (which is nothing but ignorance and you have given it the name intelligence) all these won't allow you to fully depend on your Master. Hence the struggle. If you stay with the Master in this struggle, slowly one day the Master will win. But most people when they find a struggle, they say: I came here to come out of my struggles, so let me stay alone or leave. That is dangerous. You won't have struggles but you won't progress either. So, since your intelligence gets in the way, you won't accept the Master's words totally. And the Master will create some situations where this happens. The struggle will be high. A quarrel will happen inside you. So the struggle will definitely be there but the person who is able to survive, able to continue will win the battle. Even in a real battle, who wins? The one who keeps up with the struggle without giving up correct? When you are in the struggle, slowly, definitely you will see growth. Without struggle, there cannot be growth.

Understanding Meditation Properly

In this fascinating talk, Sri Mahaprabu told us the common mistake that seekers make when it comes to meditation. And how without knowing it, they fall into the trap where meditation itself becomes an addiction and worse, gives a false sense of hope that one is progressing. He explains where effort is needed and where it is not, when it comes to Meditation.

Putting an effort to Meditate is like coming out of one's home and starting to search for it. *Or like a king who dreamt he lost everything including his palace and on waking runs about crying about his loss.* If you are in the right state of mind, this example is enough. He has not lost his home. He thinks he has lost it, and that thought makes him anxious, etc. So, he has to lose the idea that he has lost it. Therefore, effort is not needed. A right understanding is needed. For this, a sharp intelligence is needed. To come out of the sleep and the dream. A right mental attitude is needed. How do you get that? By living with a Master in Surrender. There you will get the right understanding.

The rectification is in the *Cit* portion only (*Sat Cit Anandam* is the term used to describe the Self and it loosely translates to Existence, Consciousness, Bliss). Right understanding cannot happen in *Sat* or *Ananda*. Only through *Cit Sangam* it can. Mahaprabu is also nothing but *Cit*.

Meditation can become an addiction

From young you have been craving so many things. Some things you get, and some you may not. In childhood, when you crave for something, you don't put much effort, since you are dependent. But as you grow, you will put effort into trying to get what you crave. Sometimes you get it, sometimes you don't. For example, *A boy applies for a job in a company he really likes, but he doesn't get it despite several attempts. He will think about it a lot. "I didn't get it, I didn't get it."* This affects his psychology. Another example is: *A man loves a woman a lot, but he is unable to get her. Even though he gets so many other things that he likes, this inability to get the woman he loves will have a strong impact on his psyche.* Like this, throughout our lives it becomes a habit. Longing for something and if you don't get it, you become affected.

Now the person enters the so-called 'spiritual path'. If you are not careful, Meditation or Enlightenment will become a substitute for those longings. In worldly life, the things you long for are external. So your effort is only 50% and if you don't get it, you can at least console yourself that other factors were responsible. Even then there is so much impact on the psyche. In meditation, what you are searching for is internal. There is zero dependency outside. So the proportion of your effort is 100%. Imagine the tremendous impact when you don't get what you are longing for in meditation. You will almost become a psycho. Because you will hold on to it. You will think it is your lifesaver, because you now believe that meditation is a substitute for all those things which you have rejected or which you have not received in the world. This risk is very high. If you are not alert, you won't know when you are becoming trapped by your psychology.

Meditation should not be a substitute for those things. Meditation is not something you should try for, because meditation is our natural state. Whether you are trying or not, Meditation is happening. It is in no way connected with your effort. Trying itself is wrong. It is like this: *If you are thirsty, you need not create water in this world. First, you have to find water and second, you have to drink it. That's all. And while putting the effort, you should be very clear that the effort is in finding water, not creating water. And as soon as you find it, you should drink. That's all.* This kind of awareness you should have, the understanding that meditation is a natural state, a continuous happening. It will happen. It is happening. It happened. All without your effort.

If you don't have this understanding, it will become a habit and you will get attached to it, to the point where you will sit regularly in meditation and feel good. "I have meditated today". Or there will be continuous anxiety. "I need to meditate today." or "I need to meditate more." *This is like saying repeatedly, "I need to spend more time with my children, I need to spend more time with my children." but not actually doing it.* A substitute for that is "Today I need to spend more time in meditation!"

Where is the effort needed?

Your effort is needed only to bring the Awareness not to identify yourself as a person, as a body. There you have to put in tremendous effort. Not in meditation. Mahaprabu then imitated a serious-looking seeker sitting erect: "I should feel silence. I want to feel silent. I am feeling the silence now." NO. Because, while showing interest in meditation and becoming a doer of meditation, you remain as a person. And you are telling yourself (and others) that you have done meditation. (Laughing a lot). How can "you" a person meditate? Totally wrong. Losing your personhood and not getting attached to your personhood is a basic requirement to recognize the Meditation that is happening always.

So, the effort is in bringing awareness so that we don't identify as an individual. This effort will not become a substitute for all other efforts. Here you cannot long for it. If you long for it, you will understand the foolishness of it. It would be like longing "I really don't want to think myself as a person." You will become mad. When you start feeling the ridiculousness of this, you will stop. Maybe you will get bored by it, but you won't be longing for it. You might even think "Mahaprabu keeps on telling me not to identify with a person. I am not able to avoid it. Instead let me avoid Mahaprabu!" (Laughing a lot).

So, when the effort is in bringing the Awareness not to identify yourself as a person, here there are no chances for you to get trapped by your psychology. This is where you actually are coming out of your psyche. Because as an individual you can long for anything, but you can't long for dropping individuality. Who is the one going to long and crave, if you are not identified with the individual!

This is the big danger in meditation. Getting addicted to it as a substitute for all other longings. Put up a big fluorescent sign that says "DANGER". So always try to be in Surrender. And be honest continuously. Am I identifying with a person? Yes? Then avoid it. This is what you should practice. Don't practice meditation. If you practice meditation you will start longing for it. You will go to solitary places, sit there and create another small jail around you. You will hate disturbance. You will hate the world. You will hate people. Instead of developing love, you will develop hatred. So be careful and be cheerful.

Importance of Cheerfulness

The call for Satsang came as always. When greeting Sri Mahaprabu my voice showed no enthusiasm today. Sri Mahaprabu caught it and said *"Vurchagathhoda...* With Enthusiasm! We have to develop enthusiasm and cheerfulness ourselves." This became the Satsang topic, as he spoke at length about why we aren't cheerful in general and what to do about it.

Why we are not enthusiastic

The mind will easily get dull, unenthusiastic, *Sorndhu* (in tamil). Why? Look at yesterday when you woke up. And compare that with today when you woke up. Is there any difference? No. Daily 3 times a day you feel hungry, you eat, you do the same things, you sleep and you wake up again. Go back 20 years. You did the same thing. Woke up, ate 3 times. Why won't the mind get tired? There will be fatigue.

In Mechanical Engineering, it is known that even metals have fatigue – a) due to their own weight and b) due to repeated use at specific points. They have an 'endurance limit', which eventually leads to 'fatigue failure'. If a piece of metal can get fatigue, imagine a human mind!

Enthusiasm, Cheerfulness must be developed

The difference between a metal and a mind is that the mind can refresh itself, while a metal cannot! So if you make an attempt to be cheerful, enthusiastic, you certainly will become that. Godliness comes easily to whom? To one who is ever content, grateful, cheerful. Instead if you are always sad, dull, whining about your problems, brooding internally... Godliness will not even come near you. Interestingly, if you are always crying and melting to see God, to be with God, for that person also Godliness comes easily! Both extremes bring God closer. It is the dull brooder that is so far away from God. Why? Because God is Happiness, Love, Grace. So, either come to Him with enthusiasm or with Love.

Jnana vs. Jnana infused with Bhakti

You cannot do one thing. What is that? Die.

YOU CANNOT DIE. So what is left to do? Live! So live happily, cheerfully. When Socrates was sentenced to death by poison he knew the death of the body was certain. Yet he died very cheerfully. Al-Hallaj Mansour a persian sufi poet was also executed because his views were considered anti-religious (He said 'I am the Truth'). The execution was barbaric. He was tortured and decapitated. Yet he is supposed to have borne it so cheerfully, saying: No matter what disguise you come in, I still recognize you. You gave me this body, God. Now You are taking it away. These are examples of *Jnana* infused with devotion, *Bhakti*.

SC: You regularly ask us to practice *Unarvin Thordarbu* (Being in touch with one's feeling of Existence) doing tasks while being in touch with the feeling of Existence. When I attempt to do so, at that moment there is a sense of focus, not cheerfulness. There is quietness, even seriousness in trying to be aware but not enthusiasm.

Mahaprabu: If that is the case, then you are not in *Unarvin Thodarbu*! You might think you are but you aren't. Why? Let us look at the moments that Mahaprabu has conducted *Unarvu Nilai Dhyanam* (the practice that helps us to connect with our own self). You know that at least once or twice you had the experience of tremendous happiness, or at least a serene peace. Correct?

SC: Yes certainly.

Mahaprabu: That shows that when real *Unarvin Thodarbu* was experienced, you were happy, cheerful. Which means that if you aren't cheerful, happy, you are NOT in *Unarvin Thodarbu. You are drinking something but it certainly is not the juice you think you are drinking!!*

Duality and Bliss cannot co-exist

As long as you are divided, two, *Magizchi* or Bliss or total Joy cannot exist. If you observe closely, *Unarvin Thodarbu* (getting in touch with Feeling of Existence) itself has duality. Getting in touch requires two entities. Feeling of Existence, and the Mind or attempter or attention that is trying to get in touch with it. Here is a key question: When the mind tries to reach that experience of Feeling of Existence, and in doing so begins to dissolve itself, will such a mind be cheerful or frustrated?

SC: It will experience happiness.

Mahaprabu: No. It will be dejected. Why? Because losing itself is a failure. It does not like disappearing. Yet the Mind has to fail. Only then you disappear. That failure leads to *Salippu*, dejection. So, until the mind is gone there won't be happiness. But the attempts to dissolve the mind lead to dejection, sadness. This makes the mind tired in its attempts. It resists further. What a quandary!

What to do?

You have to put in effort to continue these attempts, beyond the mind's tendencies to feel sad. If you keep on persisting in your attempts, then one day, in your disappearance there will be total *Magizchi*, Bliss. That's why I said in the very beginning, that you have to keep yourself cheerful, enthusiastic.

In all worldly matters, when you fail on the first attempt aren't you sad? No one is happy they failed. For example, *someone fails an exam, fails in his business venture, or his marriage proposal falls through. Isn't there sadness?* Yes. So, it is THAT SAME MIND that is trying for *Unarvin Thodarbu*, Awareness, being in touch with Existence. You have separated the two types of attempts (worldly vs spiritual) but it is the exact same mind. There is no such thing as worldly or spiritual. Outside vs. Inside. Naturally, that mind is going to be dejected when it does not get what it attempted to get.

OK, do you have any questions now?

SC: (Was very cheerful due to the beautiful explanation and the way Mahaprabu delivered it with so much love). No. I am happy now!

Mahaprabu: When there are absolutely no questions, no doubts, you are happy. That is the state that Mahaprabu wants to get you to. That is *Unarvin Thodarbu*. Everything else is *Thodarbu* (connection, getting in touch with) with something else, such as thoughts about *Unarvu*, ideas, opinions, and similar garbage. So yes, there will be frustration. Mahaprabu's job is not to answer all your questions, but to make the questions disappear, along with the questioner.

It is like this. *You want to go to Simla (a cool mountainous region in North India). You are on the way, somewhere in Madhya Pradesh (a very hot state in Central India). You are tired, sweating, frustrated. OK, so what does that mean? You are NOT IN SIMLA!!! Now you have two choices when it comes to your attitude. 1) Cheerfulness. I know I am not in Simla, so I need to go faster, try harder. Because I know I want to go to Simla. Or 2) Oh! I am suffering so much. This is so painful. What will I do? etc.*

Between these two attitudes, which one do you think will get you faster to Simla? Whoever is cheerful will move faster to Simla. See how SimPla (means very easily in Tamil) Mahaprabu has shown you the path to Simla! By adding just one letter P!

The only place where Godliness is revealed

Mahaprabu works for such long hours but still does not get tired or frustrated. Because he is at God's feet always. HE supplies me that boundless enthusiasm and alertness 24×7. God is ever cheerful, happy, and active. That Godly cheerfulness, where can you see? Not in a temple, Not in a human, Not in any of his Creations, for instance in the Sun. Only in the Guru. The only place where Godliness is totally revealed is in the Guru. Hence it is said Mātha (Mother), Pithā (Father), Guru (Master), Daivam (God). It shows Guru is nearest to God.

Wonderful! May things happen well.

The Problem and the Solution

Sri Mahaprabu had just spent the last hour, guiding us through *Unarvu Nilai Dhyanam* (a process that takes us inwards with ease). A stillness prevails over the room and a silence in our hearts. Mahaprabu asked us to contrast this state with the state of mind during our daily life. A single thought, that I am an individual, is running our lives. That thought knows nothing about Love or Life. Hence the miserable condition we seem to be in. He points the way out and exhorted us, urging us to make use of this rare opportunity that we have been blessed with.

The enemy is living

Individuality, the idea that you are a person is nothing but a single thought. This thought that you are a separate person is living your life. The one which does not have life is living. It does not know anything about love. It is not a true life. So there is no real happiness. Remove that enemy. Keep on trying. Keep on trying. This is the only one thing that you have to do. Life is THAT which is behind it (it refers to the idea that you are a person); behind the body and thought. But what is living is the thought that you are a separate individual. Imagine this life. No love, No joy, No happiness, No silence. You cannot attain through that thought. Or whatever you attain through that thought will not give you peace or silence.

Your reality is existing here and now, beyond the body, beyond the thought. We are not giving importance to that one. Instead, we are giving more and more importance to the body, to the thought, to the idea of an individual: I am so and so, I am like this, I should be like this, I like this, I don't like this. A strong web. This is foolishness.

Try to remember the last 10 minutes (referring to the *Unarvu Nilai Dhyanam* practice that we just had). How vital. Just I wanted to give you a taste, a glimpse. Spend more time with THAT. Allow THAT to live. THAT is real life-energy. THAT is living. It alone can live. It is the true substance that lives permanently. The body is not permanent. The thought that you are a male/female is not permanent. But the one that is existing here and now, beyond the body, beyond the thought is not bound by time; this timeless, spaceless, deathless being, it is here and now. We are missing it. Missing it continuously due to our insincerity, due to our irresponsibility, due to our indiscipline, due to our bad habits, due to our bad character. No wonder we keep missing it. We are insincere, and irresponsible habitually.

The way out

Thoughts and *Vasanas* (tendencies from many births) are the enemies that prevent you. The only way to cross them is this: Surrender, Total *Saranagathi* (surrender). *Aiiya* (Sir) I have given myself to you. I have no expectations, no opposition. If you are able to surrender like this, with no expectation and no opposition then you can kill the enemy and complete the journey. Whatever the Guru says, your mind and heart must be in line with the Master. Because you are not able to reach that which is right here, right now. Why? Due to the memory depositions (from this birth) and mental depositions (*vasanas* from earlier births which are even stronger obstacles). Your target is very near. You are very close to it. But you are unable to reach it due to these two obstacles.

So the journey must be continuous. If you leave it in between, you have to restart, because in that gap so many memories will occupy your mind and so many *vasanas* will come. It is like new growth coming out of a cut branch. You will get attracted and enjoy those new leaves and get lost. Only through Surrender without expectation or opposition, the journey can be started and continued without a break till the end. We are putting our whole life at stake in this joint venture. The Master is giving his lifetime and love for you. The time spent by him on you is priceless and has no equivalent. Precious moments. Try to understand... The target is so close to you. Yet you are struggling, even after knowing that it is there.

You have to work hard. This is your only goal. Be in total surrender. Whatever the Guru wants you to do, 100% do it. It is just you and the Guru in this life. Everything else should be made zero. Only then your memories of this birth will go, and then we can tackle the depositions from previous births (*vasanas*).

Who on this earth will fight for you like this? Think! Only the Guru. He will stand behind you throughout. No one else is even capable or interested. If you don't work hard in such a journey where a Guru is behind you at every step, then when will you ever do it?

I'm telling you, the journey has not even started yet. It will start only when you are in total surrender, with no expectation, no opposition. Only Yes, always yes, to the Master. That inner atmosphere is needed for the journey to begin.

It is a different world, the world that is waiting for you. I have enjoyed both worlds. I know the path. I am the right guide. That's why I am showing you at every step. I am showing you through the window (*Unarvu Nilai Dhyanam*). Make use of this opportunity. Human birth is a very great opportunity. Being with a Guru is extremely rare. Don't miss it. Finish it. Put a full stop to this world. Only then the other gate will be open to you. You cannot be in both worlds at the same time. Only the Guru can do that. When you become a Guru, when you become Enlightened, then God will give you the capacity to travel in both worlds. At that time you will find no difference. But till then close the door to this world. Then the door to that world will open to you. Come on. I am waiting. I am inviting you all. That's all I can say.

Only at the beginning of this journey is there a You and I. As the journey proceeds, you and I will disappear. It is a journey that has a beginning but is endless as both of them get dissolved. When both of us are dissolved, everything will be solved. Love you. Love you.

Worry

For some time, I had not spoken with Sri Mahaprabu (one-on-one), but *satsangs* were happening as always. There were a few days where I was consumed by a 'down' feeling, almost depressive. Soon my *sadhana* was affected, I did not feel like sitting for meditation, and the guilt only made matters worse. Sri Mahaprabu's call came. I told him about my situation.

Mahaprabu: The mind will trick you, saying things are going well. So, Mahaprabu at times creates a gap in contact between us (you can't call it a disconnect. It's more like a feeling in you like there is no closeness between you and Mahaprabu.) This is so that you can see the true color of your mind!

Something is spoiling the peace. The peace that you feel at the end of *Unarvu Nilai Dhyanam* is always there. (Loosely translates to "State-of-Existence meditation: A superb, guided meditation that comes from Sri Mahaprabu at times, where we always find tremendous peace at the end.) And does this peace come from the outside? No. So, it is always there, and it is always peaceful. So, who prevents you from feeling that *Amaidhi* (peace)? The thoughts that come and go in your head. So, what do you need to free yourself from? From those thoughts. How? If it is like a rope, you can cut it off. You cannot. The only way then is to ignore them. This is what Sadhu Om called "*Ulagai, Udalai, Mana ennagalai udhaseena padutharadhu.*" (Sri Sadhu Om, an enlightened disciple of Bhagavan said we need to continuously ignore, and not give any seriousness to the world, the body and all thoughts).

So at this point, what is not needed is meditation. What is needed is to ignore, deny, reject, and bypass those thoughts that have disturbed the peace. In my point of view that is true meditation. Nothing is needed to attain the peace, as it is already there. Now tell me, is this a one-hour process?

SC: No. Whenever it comes I have to keep denying and ignoring it. And denying itself implies that I'm already separating myself from them.

Mahaprabu: Yes, this is a lifetime job, this observing and denying. Whenever you succeed in doing that, you'll feel the peace! As you stay in that silence, you will get stability. For this you need patience. You have to give it time. You understand all of this, you have also experienced peace, yet in spite of it there is disturbance. Why? Because you aren't patient and giving time for it to stabilize, and in doing so, you are spoiling the progress made. So be very clear: This is what I need to do. This is what I should avoid.

SC: Many times, I feel dragged away by the current of thoughts that it is too late to do the separation and observation.

Mahaprabu: Yes, at those times you can't do it. But next time you can be prepared. This takes sincerity. It is a decision that you need to take. Silence is in-built. You should not leave it. If you leave it, what will you do? You will search for it automatically outside. You know that there is nothing outside that can give you this Silence. Still, will you keep letting it go outside? Even though it wants to go outside, will you keep going there knowing that you won't find peace?

SC: No I shouldn't. I have observed when I get this down feeling. It happens when I feel like I haven't done anything today. Just sitting not doing much. The mind has been programmed that I must do something. When the feeling of sadness gets strong, the mind resists even doing *dhyanam* and that leads to guilt and a downward spiral. So then I am wondering, What is the real purpose of man? What are we here to do???

There were a few seconds of silence and Mahaprabu said this:

The question you asked me, 'What should man do'? You should stay without the thought that you are a man. That question itself should not be there. That's what you need to do! When man was first created, what purpose would he have had? Just to exist, that's all. What is the purpose of existence? Can there be a purpose? It IS its nature to Exist. It is a play of nature.

SC: Yes, for example, a bird has no purpose. It is born and it dies.

Mahaprabu: See again you are separating it as a bird! (Laughing). Existence is flying, that's all!

SC: Right! But have read in the scriptures that *Moksha* (Liberation) is the ultimate purpose of a human birth (referring to Vivekachudamani).

Mahaprabu: Nothing at all. No purpose is there for Existence. But people have said things like *Moksha* because otherwise people won't sit down and make an attempt. People say 'I don't know myself', 'I don't know myself'. But because he IS, he is saying that. Which means he is just blabbering. You see, someone IS there to say 'I don't know myself' right? It's like having something and saying I don't have it. Observe carefully. He says 'I don't know myself', but he does not say 'I don't exist'. (Laughing). So what I'm saying is, be without this question as to what is the purpose. All purposes will be found then. This question about a purpose, who is it for? For Existence? No. It doesn't say I have forgotten my purpose. The one who is asking this question is your personhood, your mind, your brain. And it does so, using Existence.

SC: Isn't personhood or ego also Existence? Didn't Existence create the ego?

Mahaprabu: No, *Nabarthanmai* (personhood) is not Existence. The idea of a separate person is a wrong piece of information that your brain has. Whether you believe in this information or don't believe it, is Existence affected? No. You see, if there was a link between the two, then if *nabarthanmai* (personhood or ego) was affected, Existence should also be affected. Right!

Take the case of a child. There is no ego there. Isn't the child existing? Existence has created the brain and the ability to think. What was thought by that brain is not Existence. I'll ask it another way. *All food comes from where? The earth, soil. Then eat soil. Will you? Even though food comes from mud, you can't eat mud.* What you are saying is like this. Ego came from the ability to think, which came from Existence, but there is no relationship, there is no equivalency between Ego and Existence, just as there is no equivalence between soil and food. This example is not exactly logical, but it is given to show equivalence, not relevance. Normally your mind will think logically and try to match the example. But see how *Brahmam* is giving (referring to Mahaprabu talking) an example that is not exactly a logical fit, but it has an impact on your mind. You have to go beyond logic. *Food is there because of soil, but you can't treat soil as food. Ego is there because of Existence, but you can't treat Existence as Ego.* So erase this question of 'What is my purpose'. Body, Brain, and Process of thinking are all created by Existence. Except for ego or personhood (*thani nabar thanmai*).

I'll say it another way. You cannot separate the brain from Existence. You cannot separate the bones from Existence. There is integrity between the soul, body, brain, and thinking process. There is a total integration. Take out the thinking process or brain and this integrity will be lost. But if you remove the ego, will the integrity be affected? No. It has no effect. You see that it doesn't belong. This shows that Ego is not part of Existence. So you can't assume that Ego is Existence.

SC: I get this notion because it is the *Leela* (play) of Existence to lose itself. That's why I get this idea.

Once again a pause from Mahaprabu.

If you look deeply, you will see that all your attempts are to keep trying to understand Existence with your mind. But the nature of Existence is that the only way to experience it is to BE, (*Iruppu*). Not think. To put it another way, *fragrance is something that can be experienced only by smell. But you keep on trying to experience smell by touching. Then you say, I am not able to touch the smell of the rose.*

SC: Wow!! I'm using the wrong tool.

Mahaprabu: Will any book give you this example? No. IT is giving.

So, you see how your mind is continuously trying to understand Existence, even without you knowing it. Write it down somewhere. "I cannot touch the smell of the rose." Someone has to tell you, 'Raja, you cannot understand Existence'. All your efforts are a total waste. The minute you stop trying to understand it what do you think will happen?

SC: Thinking will stop.

Mahaprabu: Yes, so what will be the result? What will you feel?

SC: (after struggling a bit to envision what would happen when thinking stopped) Peace.

Mahaprabu: Here you come!! What will you feel? Peace! Now, what is missing right now? Peace! So now you know that once you stop the thinking process you will be at peace. But you are holding on to the thinking process for what? PEACE!!! You are taking yourself down the wrong route. It is a habit. It will drag you whenever you are unaware. First, for now accept that your thinking habit drags you. Like you are affected by a kind of disease. So the next time it drags you into trying to figure out Existence, suddenly when you remember that you have been dragged, where will you be? A few steps down. Again and again, keep remembering and you will come back to where you should be. Just remembering will bring you back. You don't need any effort to come back.

Here is another example: *A teenager is walking on the road. A teenage girl is drying clothes on the terrace. He looks at her but suddenly sees her father, a police inspector, also sitting on that terrace reading a newspaper. Whenever he lowers the newspaper, the boy will turn away from the girl, correct?* Just the father's presence is enough for him to turn away. See, he would have put a lot of effort to see the girl. But to turn away does he put any effort? No. It happens automatically as he is ever alert about the father, even while watching the girl. Similarly, if you are alert, as soon as you remember, you will stop thinking. So continuously try to be watchful. But you will forget. Just like the father will forget about the boy while reading some interesting news article. What I'm saying is that the effort is there only when it drags you away. It does it slowly. But once you are alert, you will come right back to the origin. Not a few steps back. Because once you are alert, you are aware, and there is no thought. So what is needed? Effort or Alertness? SC: Alertness.

So the Guru is initiating you in being alert, whenever you are missing it. What is needed is Alertness, not Effort.

Right now you are used to effort. So Alertness will still escape you. Thinking is effort, which drags you down a mile away. But the minute you become alert, you come right back to the origin. *When evening comes, it starts to get dark, and eventually there is complete darkness. But when the light switch is turned on, immediately the darkness goes away. Virutti panni pazagirka, Niruthhi pazagalai.* You are used to thinking. Not stopping.

I can put it another way also. Let's say you were able to somehow figure out using the thinking process what Existence is. The moment you find it, figure it out, at that moment what will you feel?

SC: Amaidhi, Peace.

Mahaprabu: (Laughing) So then do it without going through all this thinking! It will reveal itself anyway. Otherwise, all this thinking will make you mad.

The more alert, aware, *irundhu irundhu* (being present) you are, the ability to not go down into a loop will increase. After a point, IT will take over. IT will do its part. Once you get to Existence, you disappear. When you have disappeared, the question (referring to my original question as to what is the purpose of man) has also disappeared. IT has no right or wrong, east-west, day-night, birth-death.

You know how priceless these talks are. If you bring them into practice and experience IT, that is the greatest return.

SC: Nandri Mahaprabu.

The Real Sadhana

In this very insightful talk, Mahaprabu showed us to distinguish happenings from the knower, while beautifully explaining the reasons for doing so. He explained why we go through life in a series of pendulums of ups and downs and how to come out of it.

Happenings vs. the Knower

Two people A and B are walking on the road. Suddenly there is heavy rain. Both will get wet correct? When there is a sudden fire, and both are trapped, both are affected by the fire. Suppose A is exposed to sadness or frustration. Will B also be filled with sadness and frustration? No. Rain is real, in the sense it has existence. It is not an imaginary one. So is fire. All of those exposed to that which has real existence are affected equally. But sadness has no real existence. If it did, it would influence everyone. The one that exists here and now and in us, knows that sadness appears to be there, but it is not affected by that sadness. When that sadness goes away and happiness appears to come, the one that exists here and now is aware but is not affected by happiness either. Throughout your life, this keeps happening. Happiness and Sadness alternately affect us through so many situations, with periods of neutrality in between, but the one which is knowing simply continues unaffected by any of this.

Take the simple action of drinking milk.

I am drinking milk – This is one way to understand it.

The body is Drinking milk – This is another way to understand it.

Drinking is happening – This is yet another way.

Which of these is true? Drinking is happening.

Drinking is a phenomenon. I am the subject and Milk is the object. When the subject and object are removed, only the action remains.

Is it right to say, 'The body is drinking milk'? If you feed the same milk to a dead body, will it drink? No. Even if the body is of the same size and structure, and the mouth is open. Still, it cannot drink, even if you pour the milk into it. A live body is able to drink, and the dead one is unable to. Why?

The one which is here and now, the one which is knowing, in its presence all things are happening. This knower is not present in the dead body, so no action is possible. Therefore, ALL actions are happening just in 'its' presence.

How we get into trouble

Now, you can either focus on the happenings or you can focus on the one which is knowing. The happenings are changing continuously, but the one which is knowing never changes. When we focus our attention on the happening, there comes right-wrong, happiness-sadness, and all the ups and downs. And amongst the two, when you focus your attention on sadness or frustration your attention will be dragged more, rather than when focused on happiness. Your energy is lost more in sadness and frustration. When good things are happening in your life, beyond your control you will say 'Thank God. Because of God it happened.' But at the same time when some frustration or sadness happens, are you saying 'Because of God it happened.'? So for one-half, you are admitting God, but for the remaining 50%, you are admitting You. 'I should have not done that, I should have done this, I expected something, but I got this'... See the difference. So in these so-called negative situations, very quickly and easily you will get identified with the ego and dragged down by it. So you must be very careful. Half of you will build you up, the other half will destroy you. That is why most of the time you find that no matter how much practice you do, you feel like you are still at the same point. Because one-half constructs and the other half destructs. Construction is very slow. But destruction is instantaneous. So you should be very alert especially when frustration or sadness comes and starts to grow.

Typically when happiness comes, you will start enjoying it. For e.g. *Somehow one day you find a bag of cash in the cupboard in your bedroom. It got there without your knowledge.* Generally (I'm not talking about exceptions) the person would become very happy and say things like 'Thank God. You have finally answered my prayers for my sufferings'. Because it is beyond your control. But say, in the same house, the person had his hard-earned bag of cash in that same cupboard. The next day he wakes up to find it gone, stolen. Definitely he will be frustrated and start thinking, 'I should have locked it', 'I should have put it in the bank', etc. All kinds of 'I' come in. See how quickly we get identified. So in Happiness, we get identified and enjoy it. In frustration also we get identified but since we don't enjoy it, we try to do something, anything to come out of it.

In both cases, the problem starts in the first step itself. We get identified. We don't see it as a happening. We are not focused on the one that 'knows' that frustration is there, the unaffected one. As you have gotten identified, you say 'I must do something now', 'I must fix this situation now'. This process leads to more complications. You are developing a state of confusion. Your entire system becomes cloudy. Now it is very difficult to see the one that is 'knowing'. But it is still there. Its presence is the only reason, you even know there is a big cloud. But as you are attached to frustration and complicating it further by taking responsibility, finally you are so far away from the One that exists here and now and knows all this, that you have created a very big distance.

What to do?

So, to realize this, first you should not get identified. You should not do anything. You should focus on the one which is knowing. That is *Turiyam*. Whatever is happening, it is knowing. Since it exists every moment, it knows everything. And it never distinguishes good things versus bad things.

About Prayer:

This one that is here and now and is unaffected -from its point of view, 'You' do not exist. But from your point of you, 'You' are existing and 'IT' is existing. And you are saying 'Please help me', 'Why don't you take care of me?'. IT doesn't know about you (Laughing!). So then why prayer? To build mental strength. But you say 'My prayers aren't answered'. Who is listening to your prayer? (Laughing). From ITs point of view, you are not existing. So, your frustration also does not exist. If your frustration was real, it will influence everyone, like the Sun or Rain as I mentioned at the very beginning. So many people come to a Jnani with all their frustrations. But that never affects the Jnani. Why? It is not real.

This is the real practice

So, we should focus our attention on the one which is knowing, and not on the happenings. It is a difficult process, but we can get there if we keep on trying. Shifting our attention. This is the real Sadhana. Your attention is focused on the things that are happening but you are forgetting the one which is knowing. That knower, Seer is called *Siva, Atma, Para Brahmam*. They have given names to it. As it has no name, let us accept it as it is. The one which is existing here and now.

SC: When sadness or frustration comes, we get identified and it creates a distance from the knower. But in the opposite case, when happiness comes also we get identified and there is a distance, an equal distance. Right?

Mahaprabu: Yes, definitely. That's what I'm telling.

SC: But in one case we lose energy, but when identified with happiness we gain energy. Why is that?

Mahaprabu: Yes, you think you are gaining energy because your expectation is met. There also you are losing, building your ego, because you are not aware of the one which is knowing. That is why for those like the Buddha, there is no oscillation in them, whether frustration or happiness comes. They are always in a straight line. Ordinary people, when they get happy they start showing it, even jumping up and down. But the Buddha, imagine how much happiness he is experiencing every second. Yet he sits so calmly and quietly. See that! By your standard, how much he should jump in joy! Take the case of Osho, he encourages disciples to dance in joy. But he himself doesn't. Even if he does, it is a slight movement. Even though he is enjoying the ultimate, supreme happiness, there is no dance. Because they remain as the one that is unaffected.

So what we have to do is, instead of focusing on your state of mind, you have to be alert. Otherwise you will quickly drop your sadhana. Shift your attention to the One which is knowing everything. In a 24-hour day, if you draw a curve of your mental state, it will be full of ups and downs. How do you know this? There is something that knows this. That thing which knows, Its line is a straight line throughout the day. So, both lines are available. Which one do you want? The one that goes up and down and torments you? Or the straight line, like the Buddha's? Definitely the straight line. That is why people who are in the ups and downs are attracted to the ones who are in the straight line (*jnanis*). The reverse is never true. The ones who are stable are never attracted to, never influenced by those in the curves going up and down. This itself indicates which is real and which is apparent.

This is the real practice. The core practice is this. Everything else, chanting, meditating, are all time-pass. What to do? You are in the curve. The Master has to join with you in the curve. He will appear to rise with you, and appear to fall with you, but he is always in the straight line. When you first meet the Master, your curves are steep with huge highs and lows. He gives you the feeling that he is also coming with you, even though he really is unaffected. As time goes on, he reduces the amplitude and the frequency of the waves. Slowly, over time, your curved line will become straight. The Straight line is the Master and Curves is the disciple. Straightening the curve is the *sadhana*.

So, from this moment, shift your attention from what is happening, to the one which is knowing, which is here and now. You have to succeed in this. This is the Sadhana and it is in your hand only.

Mahaprabu also spoke about Surrender:

What are you surrendering to the Master? You are surrendering the one which does not exist. When you say you are surrendering, it means you should give something. You are giving the one that doesn't exist. You are giving 'nothing' but getting 'everything'. To give this 'nothing', you find it so difficult!

Moment to moment, practice it

Mahaprabu ended the session as usual by praying to all the *Brahma Jnanis* to bless us. As he raised his hands while saying *Vazga Valamudan* (may you live prosperously) he stopped midway and said: Even as my hands are going up in the air, the one which is here and now is knowing it. The attention is focused on that which is here and now and knowing. But what do we do? You will forget that and fall for the body action, fall for the words, fall for the feeling. All those are there: Body action, words and feelings. All of these are there when I say the blessings. But the fourth one is there!!! That you forget. You should know the one which is knowing. That is the meaning of knowing yourself. One portion of you should always know that 'the knower is there'. Then slowly, slowly the body's actions will reduce, words will reduce and feelings will merge (between disciple and Master). After that point, this *'Vazga valamudam'* will not be said. Just the presence becomes the blessing. So give more importance to the knower. That is the real blessing. Remain as that. That is the powerful blessing. These words, these body actions are not the real blessing. From this moment, make this the real Sadhana. Shift your attention towards the one which is knowing everything, which is present every moment. As it is present every moment, it knows everything. This practice is possible only in a human body and that too only when the body is alive. Saying this, Mahaprabu continued the blessings after which the Satsang ended.

The 3Ds

You are living a lie. You are Not. Something else Is. In this destructible body, there is an indestructible Brahman. You aren't there, I am not there. You are living a lie. You have been living a lie for many births. And the lie only gives you suffering. Now you know this is a fact. Shouldn't you take corrective action?

What is needed is this

You know you are living a lie. For change to happen in you, a strong DECISION is needed that I will no longer let this lie rule my life. Only then can you alter your DESTINY. In between Decision and Destiny is one more thing. Strong DETERMINATION, that no matter how many times I fail, I will not give up, I will not deviate from my DECISION. This is a basic rule of 3D's. As you want to change your Destiny, you have to change the Decision. And to bring the Decision into action, to reach the Destiny, what is needed is Determination. In these 3, only Destiny is a single word. The other two need the word STRONG as a prefix. Strong Decision and Strong Determination.

Without doing this how will anything happen? First you must make a strong Decision. Then you must change your whole life accordingly. Then you are on the track. That is the only way. Otherwise, you will be getting in and out of the track continuously and make no progress.

You are Not. Something else Is.

In this destructible body, there is an indestructible Brahman. You aren't there, I am not there. Isn't this a wonder? All these years we have been living as though 'I' exist. Now you understand that you are not. And that something else is living. *It is like a Mother who loves her son and has brought him up well. The son finds out one day that he is not her original son, but an adopted one. And he hears that she has a real son. Won't he be curious to meet him? Find out all about him. Similarly, a false king who has been ruling the country for a long time finds out that the real King, a great one is there. Won't he be curious to see him?* Like that you should also yearn to find out who you really are. I am not. Something else is. I have no experience of THAT. I only have an experience of me, a male, a separate person. And the experience of me is not even pleasant, not sweet, and I know it is not going to continue. So all the more shouldn't I want to know my true nature? See how many people even after coming to the *Atma Jnana* (knowing oneself) path are still holding on to themselves. It takes tremendous Determination, *Vairgyam*.

We are not this body. We are not a separate individual. In this destructible body, there is an indestructible part that is said to be of great Arivu (Knowing, Consciousness), great *Amaidhi* (Peace) great *Anandam* (Joy, Bliss). We should experience it and change our entire life accordingly. He who tries for it is a Yogi. The benefit of being a Yogi is that he can also be a *Bhogi* (enjoyer). But he who is just a *bhogi* will remain a *bhogi*.

We should treat this as an adventure, as our only job. As you allow it and allow it, you will know about it. Know about real life. All these years even though you have obstructed it so much, it has been coming along throughout.

This *ahandai*, ego is a thought. A thought that you are a person. Does that make you a person? No. For example, You can think you are a lion. Does that make you a lion? No. The man that you are, just because you think you are a lion will not become a lion. If you think you are a Tree, you won't become a tree. Just because you think you are a stone, you will not become a stone. Just as this is true, the Brahman that you are, just because you think you are an individual, does not make you an individual. You are still Brahman alone. If you agree with the example I gave you, you have to accept this as well.

You are a lie. Something else is the Truth. First this has to be clearly accepted in your thought, otherwise you won't even turn to towards Brahman. That is why *Shravanam* (listening to the words of the wise) is important. As a human you have the ability to logically analyze and understand things. While you are sleeping, something runs the body automatically; the lungs, the heart, etc. In your absence the body is still running. This means other than you, some force is activating the body. That same force wakes you up after sleep. Not you. Having understood this, who will yearn to find out about that force? He who is tired of the worldly life. There are two possibilities: Either he should be tired or we need to create that tiredness in him. The Guru helps in both cases. As he listens to the Guru and acts accordingly, he will realize how tiring it is to live as a lie.

Only a Lie can tire you

What will make you tired? Only a lie. The Truth will never make you tired. Only a real flower will give you a fragrance. A fake flower, a plastic flower will tire you, as there is no fragrance. And yet you keep staring at the plastic flower from far and think you are enjoying a real flower. So the Guru keeps bringing the plastic flower close to your nose. (Laughing!!) He says, "There are real flowers that have fragrance. What you have been staring at is all plastic." But since you are involved in the world and totally identified, even if I bring a real flower to you, you still treat it as plastic!

Love, Awareness, Feeling of Existence

A disciple was serving coffee. Sri Mahaprabu noticed that she was doing it mechanically, without awareness. That spurred this beautiful talk about how we live entire lives without becoming aware of ourselves, aware of the feeling of Existence. How this is related to Love. And what is the only way to regain this awareness: Through Surrender.

Attention on the Feeling of Existence

From young we have craved and struggled for many things. As a child we craved toys, chocolates, ice creams. As a youth it was sensual pleasures, fancy shoes etc. Then it was career, house, car etc. One by one they have gone away. Similarly in spirituality you start to focus your attention on the Awareness, the feeling of Existence, the formless. It is formless but is not a void. It is full of love, with energy, with grace, with light. When you focus your attention on this feeling of Existence, slowly your struggle with other things will disappear. This is the only way.

When your attention is diverted and focused on this Feeling of Existence ALWAYS... (Mahaprabu repeated the slow movement of his hand as he said the word ALWAYS, to show that even that movement should not distract you from the attention on the Feeling of Existence). ALWAYS means NOW. You must give this much value, to THIS ONE, the one which is living in this body, the one which is full of love.

Feel Love. You know its power

See, you feel LOVE in your body, Right? Where do you feel love? In the leg? In the bones? In the flesh? Hairs? You may love your flesh or hair. But love is not in the flesh or hair. And yet love is there. That is the Center. Focus your attention on that Loving Center. Don't imagine Atma, Brahman, Consciousness. You don't know about those things. Feel that Center. You already know the power of Love. When you touch someone with love, you know the feeling. When you are touched by someone lovingly, you know that feeling. Someone even looking at you lovingly, you know that feeling. You know the power of Love. Love may be shown through the eyes but Love is not in the eyes. A wonderful thing is available in us named Love. That Love is the entry pass to meet God. Give more and more importance to that. Love exists in you and Existence exists in you through Love. Nothing else needs to be learned or imagined. God, Atma, all these are mere words for you. On the other hand, you already know the feeling of Love. Give importance, give attention to it. Very quickly it will take you to the Center.

The nucleus is the Center of an Atom. But when you look into the Nucleus, that Center has another Center called the Nucleolus. Similarly, Love is the Center. But that Love has another Center. When you catch, when you hold on to Love, it will take you to the inner Center, which is the root; the connection with the Eternal. When you are able to find and reach that root, then fear will disappear. Joy and ecstasy abound. To reach that root, Love is the route.

So give more and more importance to the feeling of Love. The only thing that is freely available in the universe, which cannot be exhausted, and grows when it is given is LOVE. When your heart is completely filled with Love, Enlightenment is bound to happen. In the process of Loving, in the process of feeling the Love in you, your Ego is bound to disappear. That no ego state is called the state of Enlightenment. Slowly, try to bring it.

First, learn to love You

For example, see how important your Neck is. It connects the body to the head and the brain. The esophagus and trachea, passages for food and air are in the neck. Thyroid and Parathyroid glands are there in the neck. At the back, the spinal cord goes through the neck to connect to the brain. Imagine a life without the neck, where your head is stuck to your torso. You wouldn't be able to turn it. This neck is a beautiful creation of God. Mahaprabu held his neck with both hands and said: Have you touched your neck like this with love and gratitude, at least once in your entire life? We are touching a dog with love. But our own neck? The neck is just one portion. How many such portions are in our body? First, express your love for yourself. Start there. And whenever you express love, do it with Gratitude. When you do that, you are expressing love for God. And then express your love throughout the Universe. In your life, at least one time have you conveyed your love to the Whole Universe? 'I love the whole universe. The universe has given me a place here.' Have you ever done this? But you have love in you. Not showing love is also an offense! You have an inexhaustible source of Love. Even when everything is lost, this source will still be available, even in your last moment, even if the body is about to perish. At that moment also, if you express love, it will give you a continuity. That invisible continuity is love, that invisible continuity is God.

I am not asking you to express your love by hugging a stranger. Because it may not be reciprocated and some other things may happen! In each and every action try to bring love. Even if you have scolded someone, if you are unable to give love at the time, as soon as it is over go back and send love towards him. That is sowing the seeds of love after the thunderstorm.

Love is the feeling that will take you to the Feeling of Existence. Love is the nucleus, Feeling of Existence is the nucleolus. Love is the stem and Feeling of Existence is the root. As there is a root, the stem is. As there is the stem, the root is. The whole thing is called the plant. You cannot separate them. Bring your attention to the Feeling of Existence, that you Exist. No one needs to tell you that you Exist. Your body or thoughts aren't needed for that. Who created that? Who are we? The body or the Feeling of Existence (*Unarvu*). The body comes from the uterus and goes to the grave. Will this Feeling of Existence go with it? What will happen to it? Where is Love, Yearning, etc that is in us? Where is it? Is it in the body? Or is it in that feeling of Existence? (Singing Sadhu Om's Song: *Ini yenum enni yedhu naan, endru idhayaasanathil amaradho. At least hereafter, will I come to know who I am and rest in the heart*)

The biggest mistake thus far

If I am NOT the body, and I am the Feeling of Existence, then all my assumptions so far have been totally wrong. For the last 50 years. What a terrible mistake. You've been doing so many things thinking you are the body. As a slave to 'I', having worked for it all these years, doing everything to protect the 'I', to protect a total lie. *For example, you believe someone is a good person. But you find out he has been betraying you all the while. How bad will you feel?* Similarly, having found out that you are not this body, and that the ego has been destroying you with this identification, how much worse should you feel? You feel bad for small losses. This here is the biggest fraud, the biggest loss, the biggest miscalculation. How bad should you feel? Compared to this betrayal, all the losses you have ever had don't matter at all. Those are irrelevant. And what is the price that you have paid for the biggest mistake you have committed? What is the price? Loss of freedom. What is the result? All your suffering. But by the grace of God and his nature to forgive, you are getting another chance. He has put you here.

This Feeling of Existence, *Unarvu* is the only real reason you are able to exist and sense your body and the world around you. Your body functions because of it. So, more than the body, more than the world you should focus your attention on this Feeling of Existence. Then you would not suffer and complain about all the little things that affect the body (mind included). The body has a thousand issues that will drag you down. The world has countless issues that will drag you down. Both only trap you.

Awareness on Awareness

So no matter what you are doing, keep on bringing awareness to that Feeling of Existence. You will miss it many times. You will get TIRED. Why? Because you haven't TRIED it so far (laughing!) But don't let that stop you. Keep on trying. Keep on trying. Feel your own Existence. That is all I'm asking you. I'm not asking you to enquire 'Who Am I' continuously or chant some mantra continuously. Wherever you go or whatever you do, 'You' (referring to *unarvu*, Feeling of Existence) are there. Without 'You' it is not possible. Just recall and confirm moment to moment. YES, I AM HERE. YES, I AM HERE. Try it sincerely. For 12 months try it without missing a single day. This year will be the most wonderful in your life.

Mahaprabu looked at a disciple and said: Your hands are clapping right now, but your attention is not on the Feeling that you Exist. Disciple: I was thinking! Mahaprabu: Thinking is not going to give you anything. Instead of *thanking me* for catching you unaware, you are saying you are *thinking.* In your mind you are a seeker of Truth, analyzing what the Master says. Who asked you to think? I am asking you to FEEL your own Existence. In fact, this entire talk came from you. I saw you serving coffee without Awareness. That's where this talk is coming from.

Wherever you are, whatever you do, even speaking with others, keep the attention on that feeling of Existence. It is there.

If you are unable to feel it, close your eyes and keep your hands on your chest. Not your dress. On your skin. Feel that touch. Feel the air coming and going. Feel the lungs expand and contract. Which is feeling all these things? That is the Feeling of Existence. Something that is aware of all this; that exists in the body but is beyond the body.

Only through Surrender can this be done

Even after knowing all this, it appears very difficult because your head is filled with so many things at the surface as well as in its very depths. Filled with information about external things. So it keeps pushing you out. Even thoughts about spiritual practice are dangerous. They keep reminding you, making you merely think: 'We should not give importance to ego, we should not give importance to individuality' etc. It will never work. It is the ego doing it. You cannot get rid of the ego on your own. If it feels like it is happening, then that is done by the ego. That is why even though you have been trying for so many years the ego has not left you. Because you firmly believe that through your efforts you can attain something. Only through Surrender, especially in situations created by nature or by the Master, when you do not give importance to the ego, only then the ego weakens. Not giving importance to the ego when it rises, is the way to drop the ego. Just observing it and being in Surrender is the way. Then you are a clean glass. Existence will shine through it clearly. No barriers of thoughts, feelings, etc. That is why Bhagavan Osho says 'Can you be headless?' Only then can you be a disciple. Until then you are merely qualifying to be a disciple. Only when you are headless, communion is possible. When communion happens, there is a possibility for the Truth to enter. Bhagavan Ramana Maharshi also said, 'If one serves a master for 12 years continuously without a sense of doership, then he attains the Grace of the Guru.'

Stay in surrender. Come let us play the game of master and disciple, in the playground of Surrender. I am always waiting in the playground, but you are at home. I am inviting you to the ground, but you are telling me 'Come, let's play at home where I'm comfortable!'

Manifestation of Sat Cit Anandam

Background: Some of us wondered why at times Mahaprabu melts in Devotion and urges us to Surrender while at other times he urges us to practice Awareness every moment. As if he were reading our minds, the following words came out of him one day.

The 3 Aspects of the Supreme

There are 3 aspects of the Supreme indicated by the words Sat, Cit, Anandam. These 3 aspects of the Supreme Power cannot be separated. And then there is Nama and Rupa: Name and Form. We should put aside Names and Forms since they keep changing. Our attention needs to be on the three. Sometimes Anbu (Love or Ananda) dominates. At that point Arivu or Cit takes a back seat, so to speak. Similarly when Arivu (Cit) dominates, Anbu will take a back seat. When Arivu and Anbu both take a back seat, it is the Sat Nilai: State of Existence.

When Mahaprabu is dominated by Love and Ananda, his talks focus on Devotion. He asks us to give importance to Devotion. (Feels like this is a response to a question that has been with me for long: Why does Mahaprabu sometimes say Devotion is the way and sometimes say Awareness is the way? Thank you Mahaprabu.) When Cit, Arivu raises its head, Mahaprabu talks about Awareness. And when it goes really high it comes out as Unarvu Nilai Dhyanam (a guided meditation that comes out of him sometimes). At some point, both Cit and Ananda fade into the background and what remains is a total Nisabdham, Silence. In total Silence can you feel Love and Arivu interfering? No.

So these 3 aspects are inseparable. They just manifest in different ways at various times. So it is not either or. THAT which you are trying to attain is expressing itself as Love sometimes, as Awareness sometimes, and as total Silence sometimes. Therefore the approach to feeling it should also correspondingly be in sync. So no confusion at all.

Celebrate, Be Happy

We are proceeding on the right track. Mahaprabu repeated this a couple of times. (Referring to the path of Atma Jnana and having a Guru in this life).

Celebrate it. Be very happy and grateful. How many people are not even on the track? And there are crores who don't even know that there is a track. Compared to them, God has selected you and put you on the track. Are you showing him your gratitude and happiness: "I am on the Track. That itself is enough God." Do you have that attitude? In every small thing, you need to show gratitude and happiness. If you are not happy now, will you be happy when you attain the so-called destination? No. IT will know that no matter what IT gives, you are not going to be happy. Then IT stops giving. See how important that attitude is!

Nee jnanathha adaiyaharadhukkana padhaila illa. Nee payanikkira paadhayae Jnana padhai dhan.

You are not on the path to Jnana where there is something called Jnana at the end to attain. The path itself is Jnana.

The path itself is made of Jnana. Just walking it will give you it. Day to day, moment to moment is the practice. Second to second, IT moves. Being with it is the key. Not doing something now outside of it, to finally get it at a later point.

Note: This reminds me of the four *chilra kasu* (pennies) talk he gave long ago. Keep on collecting the 4 pennies at every step by being aware, conscious. In the last step also there are 4 pennies only. There is no pot of treasure in the end. If you miss collecting those 4 pennies at every step, then in the end you will end up a pauper. But if you earned those 4 pennies at every step, the last 4 will put you over the top!!!)

Nature and Surrender

Sitting under an Almond tree, Sri Mahaprabu showed us the greatness of the Supreme Power and how insignificant we are. Being in unity with Nature is very important. As the Guru is in union with nature, be in unity with the Guru, he taught us.

Glory of the Universe

During Satsang under the large almond tree, Mahaprabu pointed out how from the ground, water and nutrients are sucked upward, against gravity, and sent all the way to the tip of every leaf no matter how spread out it is. And this is happening continuously. Not only that, there is a certain size, shape, and texture to the tree which we call the Almond tree. Where is that information stored? That should have been in the seed. But the seed is so small. Where was it before the seed? It should have been in the state before the seed, which is the flower. So in the flower there is information as to what the seed should contain. But where was the information about the flower? Eventually you can trace it back to the first seed. Before that it was just information. So in this *prapancham* (universe), all information was there prior to materialization. Including what we call humans. Even if it (nature) wipes out all matter, all living things, because the information is there, it can still produce life.

Just realizing and reflecting on this greatest Brahmandam that enlivens billions of living things, and all matter, Panchabootha: Space, Air, Fire, Water, Earth, you will become humble, silent and surrender to the Supreme. But we don't give any thought to all this. Our attitude is 'Do you know who I am? See what all I have done!'. And we focus on the most trivial things. See, space is the most subtle, most limitless, all-pervasive thing we can perceive. So, that which created Space and all of this universe with its living and non-living things, imagine how great and all-pervasive that Atma is. That Brahman is. Where it will take things you and I don't know. If IT decides to remove humans, you and I will not be there to even talk about Atma Jnanam. All this talk is useless. Therefore, just keep on being in tune with nature, living in close unity with Nature *(Iyarkai oda ondri vaazanum)*, only then certain truths will reveal themselves in you. First live in close unity with the Guru. That is Satsangam. Because he is already one with Nature. Therefore certain Truths are known to him which is why he is at peace always. So to attain peace and happiness, be in Surrender. Surrender will happen only when you realize the Brahmandam that created all this and you.

In front of that Intelligence (which is in you), your ignorance cannot win. Ignorance can never know Intelligence. So as you keep feeling that presence in daily life, that intelligence will begin to shine. And whenever ignorance comes in front of you, that intelligence will correct it. Over time the mind will stop. This practice must be done in daily life. Don't entertain the idea that you are in an ashram and are allocating time for Dhyanam when you sit. That is a part of Maya too. Your mind will be quiet then, and disturb you at all other times.

Sleep, Attention, Atma - Part 1

> Sri Mahaprabu spoke about the importance of going beyond Sleep. It is a prerequisite for knowing oneself, he says. Who is Sleep for? Can there be an awareness of sleep? All these questions are meticulously answered. In fact, he asks the questions as usual, and answers them himself.

Sri Mahaprabu called me around 2:30 AM! The topic of sleep came up. In his characteristic style he asked 'Have you given rest to the body?' (Mahaprabu never ever says things like 'Did you sleep' etc. as the sentence makes no sense. Neither is there a 'you' nor is there 'sleep'. There is only the body and it rests when it needs to. Please read the other talks on Sleep and you'll see why Sleep is a habitual made-up concept without any basis in reality). I replied, 'Almost slept'. What came out of him was a very insightful talk with a clear guiding path forward.

Mahaprabu: You have to drop sleep. There is a state called Sleepless-Sleep. You see, we all ARE. We Exist. This Existence is 24 Hours. This is our true nature. Call it X. All the *Jnanis* and the *Vedas* have been saying that IT is a state that always exists. Therefore, does X have sleep?

SC: No.

Mahaprabu: Yes, sleeping is not a characteristic of this. So who is sleeping? It is something else. OK. What is that we are trying to feel, trying to attain?

SC: X.

Mahaprabu: Yes, and that X is that which never sleeps, always aware. Now tally, and correlate these two. We are trying to attain X, and X is always there, doesn't sleep, always aware. So how we should be?

SC: We should be like X, without sleep.

Mahaprabu: Yes! This is the problem, not just for you, but for everyone. OK, so if only from 10 AM to 11 AM you experience X, will it be enough? No. So when will you know for sure and experience X that never sleeps? Only if you personally experience it when the body is asleep. Only then you will say X never sleeps, something else is sleeping. Therefore, to experience the sleepless nature of X even when the body is sleeping, you have to be awake. Now what is that 'You' referring to? Careful, there are 3 things. Body (Y) is sleeping. Body doesn't care whether there is an X that never sleeps or not. X never sleeps. X also does not have a need to realize that it doesn't sleep. X doesn't need to know. Body doesn't care to know. There is a 3rd thing. That intention to know X, I am saying 'You', is not *nabarthanmai* (ego), but *Gavanam*, Attention. Not ego because when you cross the body and head towards X, you have to drop the ego. Once you go past the ego, the attention will be there, right? Yes. Is that attention separable from you? No. It is that Attention that needs to know that Y (Body) is sleeping, X is awake. Now this attention is related to what, its origin is what? X or Y?

SC: X

Mahaprabu: See what a game this is. The attention that comes out of X, does not know that X is always awake, eternal. It (X) exists all the time but it is not felt. What is the reason? Lack of attention. So how can you fix it? Only by *Gavanam*, Attention. So then are Attention and Sleep antonyms or synonyms? Antonyms. Therefore, do you have to drop sleep or not? You have to drop sleep. So, you the ego need to do what with sleep? You have to drop it. Without dropping it you cannot attain. So, sleep should not be a big deal for you going forward. If you are really interested in attaining this Truth, where you should not focus, and for what you should not give importance? For Sleep. That's all.

Imagine you are a scientist who is observing closely something very interesting. Will he give importance to sleep? No. At least he can afford to say 'Let me sleep a bit'. But you are a scientist observing the one that doesn't sleep! Can you say 'Let me sleep a bit.'? Here also you can make excuses, but the exercise will not be complete!

SC: This may be an excuse, but after some time the body seems to give up and fall asleep.

Mahaprabu: That is not a problem. The body is not all related here. Attention is no way related with the body.

SC: In theory yes, but for me, in practice they both appeared to be tied together.

Mahaprabu: Yes, Yes. It appears that way. But ask yourself. Is attention related to body?

SC: No, in fact when I am attentive, there is no ego, neither an idea of the body is felt.

Mahaprabu: Yes, that is what I'm saying. Your worrying about sleep has no meaning. Attention is not related to Ego. Attention is not related to the body. So, does Attention need to worry about the body?

SC: No. Which means, that which is worried about the body and sleep is something else.

Mahaprabu: That's it (Laughing). Who else! Mr. Ego is the one worrying. So, understanding this, you have to go beyond it. You have to counsel yourself. Attention is inborn. Ego is not inborn. Attention's focus is on X. If the body rests, Attention is not concerned. You have to clear this stage. This, only you can do. Since you are the individual (ego) who has the problem! (Laughing).

SC: This attention, since it belongs to X, can we take X as *Sat*, and Attention as *Cit*?

Mahaprabu: No, we cannot split *Sat* and *Cit*. It is *SatCitAnandam*. We say it as 3 things (Laughing), but it is one. Wherever *Cit* is, *Sat* is behind. For example, I'm saying *Sat* as X, *Cit* as Y, *Ananda* as Z. But you can't take *SatCitAnanda* as X+Y+Z. I say them as X, Y and Z as you know those 3 words as separate words. Based on your understanding I'm saying *SatCitAnanda* is the combination of X, Y, Z. But you can't take it as X+Y+Z. I'm saying *SatCitAnanda* is really W! (Laughing).

Continued

The talk continues. It is simply split into two because from here on Sri Mahaprabu did not talk about Sleep, but rather stepped back and looked at the whole picture, and what needed to be done. It is a pure joy to read.

Sleep, Attention, Atma - Part 2

Sri Mahaprabu dives deep into a discussion about Atma, Attention, Feelings, Thoughts, Body and the World. It resulted in a brilliant unraveling of these various layers and what one needs to do to unentangle oneself from the traps in these layers. A must-read, especially for an advanced seeker. Please make sure to read Part 1 of this talk before reading this.

The Importance of Attention

SC: I learnt something valuable today that while am not the ego, and that *Atma* is a mere concept to me, I realize that there is an 'Attention' that is separate, and that I am the Attention. It is self-evident to me (i.e. it is not a means of knowledge). I'd even say I am the Attention. (When the letter X is used below it refers to that which we all ARE. We Exist. The Existence that is 24 Hours. Our true nature. Atma, etc.)

Mahaprabu: Definitely. Only with that Attention can you feel Atma. You have to hold on to Attention strongly.

See, Attention is different, Feelings are different. Below Feelings is *Atma*. Thoughts are different. The Body is different. The World is different. Of all of these, which is the closest to *Atma*, X? Attention. Think of all these as layers covering each other for example, with X at the nucleus. The first layer surrounding it is Attention, then Samskaras, Feelings, Thoughts etc. When the Attention expands outward what happens? It will go towards Feelings, Thoughts, Body and World. But if it becomes highly focused and shrinks (*Odungual*), what will it reveal? *Atma* X!

In the world layer will there be emotion? No. Thought? No. Body? No. For example, if the Body has a headache will the world have a headache? Like that, each of these are only in its own layer, but Attention alone can go to all layers when it expands. Where does Attention come from? X. That means X, *Atma* is in all layers, in the form of Attention, but not in its concentrated form. I'm saying all this for your understanding. Watch closely. A disturbance in the body won't affect the world. But the disturbance in the body impacts Attention. Similarly, a disturbance in any layer disturbs Attention. When attention is disturbed, who is disturbed? X, *Atma*!

SC: But *Atma* cannot be disturbed right?

Mahaprabu: That is only theory to you. That is not your experience. *Atma* cannot be destroyed is true. But it does get disturbed. That disturbance does not destroy *Atma*, but that disturbance is the real motivation for *Atma Jnana*. What is the most peaceful thing? *Atma*. Attention comes from *Atma*. When Attention gets impacted in all layers, Attention gets disturbed. As a result, *Atma* is disturbed. But since *Atma*'s nature is peace, when it feels the disturbance, it becomes the motivation for it to regain peace. That's why you want to sit and meditate! If Attention was not disturbed at any level, and *Atma* was therefore undisturbed, will *Atma* ever sit and meditate? Will there be any motivation? You see, this disturbance is the real motivation! It gets the sense that going outwards leads to disturbance.

All this in concept is OK. But in practical terms, you have to ensure that the Attention is not disturbed in any level. No matter what the outer situation (world), or physical situation (body, thoughts, feelings) is, you have to recollect that Attention is separate and not fall for the trap 'I am disturbed'. Here is where Surrender is a tremendous help. Surrender gives immediate peace and calms the disturbance. Since X's nature is also peace, Surrender leads to strength. You will be in the same world and body but with more strength. Though there is a disturbance in any layer, as you have developed strength, the disturbance will not disturb you (Attention). When Attention is not disturbed one bit, X is not disturbed one bit, everything will happen perfectly as you operate in the world. This is *Sagajam*, *Sagaja abhyasam* (a continuous state of silence throughout daily activity). When there is no need for Attention to function in the world, body, thought, etc. it will shrink and stay in X where it will feel a total peace, a total strength. Complete rejuvenation. Everything will be shut off, but Attention will be there with X. Then you will realize this Sleepless-Sleep.

So see, what is it that makes all these layers glow? *Atma*. To be more accurate, the Attention that comes from *Atma*. So unless the Attention goes to those layers, they won't even exist for you. See, this is how you can shut down the world by withdrawing Attention from those layers.

SC: Yes, they are dead matter. Attention enlivens them.

Mahaprabu: Yes, that's why Sadhu Om says '*Vizippil Ulagai, Udalai Mana Ennagalai udhaseena paduthhi pazaga vendum*' (Always ignore, treat as inconsequential, World, Body, and Thoughts). You are the one showing light on them. Turn off the light everywhere and see the origin of the light. Always staying in X is one extreme. Always leaving X and staying in all other layers is another extreme. You go to *Atma*, experience X, and then come to all layers. Only one thing: The disturbance created in each and every layer should not disturb you. That ability you can develop. Because it is possible. Despite all the disturbances in all the layers, it is possible to stay undisturbed. That is your potential, your capacity. But right now it is not like that. Regaining your potential, your capacity is enlightenment.

Have you heard this anywhere? X is traveling at 100 Kmph in heavy traffic while talking to you. In between when the line was cut with you, I spoke on 6 calls. Yet when we resume, the conversation resumes exactly where we left it. Because IT is doing everything.

SC: Yes Mahaprabu. And unless X involves itself in all layers, this kind of message won't come out. (referring to the fact that if Mahaprabu sat in silence, in X, without going outward, the world would not come to know of these insights that are pouring out right now)

A brilliant example

Mahaprabu: Yes, you have to have the experience of X and travel in all layers. *Like a spider. It weaves the web, stays in the center of the web and it can go to extremes also. Sometimes it will also tactfully use just a single strand, to hang outside the web. And the beauty of the spider is that it weaves the net to catch what? Small Insects. But the spider even though it is a small insect itself, it never gets trapped. It will walk and dance on the spider web.* (SC: What a beautiful example. I have heard the spider example in the scriptures but never ever like this). So, who created the Spider?

SC: Atma, X.

Mahaprabu: Such a great technology of the spider, weaving different sizes of webs, in the right places, travelling across the webs, outside them, hanging from them, not getting trapped in them, so much intelligence is in the spider, therefore that intelligence is in-built into X. Since X is pervading all, this intelligence is everywhere, in everything, in everyone. But you can see the spider explicitly where? In the Guru. He will mix with everyone in the world but won't get trapped. Try to be a spider. It never goes to extreme i.e. *never does it always stay spinning web, nor does it always stay in the web. When there is no need, it doesn't spin, when there is a need it spins.* But look at people practicing *Atma Jnana.* They make up an artificial lifestyle that becomes rigid.

See, that Attention can abide in X or expand totally. You said *Atma* cannot be disturbed. I'm saying *Atma* 'can' be without being disturbed but right now it is not. See how subtle the difference is.

Now you need to take this clarity you got and move to the next step. This is hearing or listening, *Shravanam.* How long will you be in *Shravanam?* Every now and then keep remembering. The inside work has to keep on going. Take the members in the family. You think they are continuously enquiring or interested in enquiring about their real nature. If you sit with them and keep talking (for example I'm saying), will you be able to do *Mananam?* No. *Like in a hostel when everyone is studying for the exam, you also will feel like studying. Instead, if you come home, the atmosphere is the opposite. All are watching TV, a cricket match. Slowly you'll get pulled in.* Similarly, *Mananam* can be done regularly, only if you are in *Satsang* with the Guru regularly. Otherwise, you will let what you heard slip away. In *Satsang* you will be in touch.

SC: Throughout the day the thought of 'I am not the body' keeps coming. It is increasing day by day.

Mahaprabu: What a blessing that is. Of so many crores of people, who has this blessing? You should take it as a huge blessing (*asirvadham*). God has selected me out of so many and given me the opportunity to think of him 24×7, what a tremendous grace is operating. If you keep on sensing it, will you lose strength? Will you be frustrated? If you are frustrated, then you aren't sensing it. A very great work is happening. Move to *Nidhidhyasanam.* See, disturbance will exist in all layers. You cannot quit the layers. But you know that you have the capacity to be undisturbed. You don't have that ability now, but you CAN develop it. For now, don't go to places where you can be disturbed. Try to be in Surrender. That will give you strength. Instant strength. Instant power. The disturbance will minimize. Come to X. Stay in X. Then go to a low-risk disturbance. See if you can be without disturbance there. Then come back to X. This is how you attain *Jnana.* Then you attain *Sagaja Jnana.*

The things I'm telling you now are what I knew in 2003. I had this clarity then. Not something I got yesterday. I'm just driving a car now at 100km (Laughing). I'm sharing what happened in 2003. But it's so fresh. It is ancient, but always fresh as Osho says. What I'm telling you now, which is theory to you, when you work and bring it to experience, then you will attain *moksha,* come out of this curse. Whether we come out of this curfew or not, we should come out of this curse, since this curfew also is part of the curse! (referring to the Covid lockdown).

The more earnestly someone asks, the more it comes from me. The next step will be even deeper. Right now, it is like a theory for you. As I speak it will turn into Experience for you, without your effort. You will shrink in X. That is going to happen.

Attention, Love and Life

What is Attention? Why it is extremely important to be aware of Attention. Are Attention and Love related? Can they be separated? How does one become Attentive continuously? All these topics are shared by Sri Mahaprabu.

As *satsang* was about to start, Sri Mahaprabu noticed a disciple's attention drifting and pointed it out to him. Mahaprabu spoke about this.

Attention

A single thought can quickly multiply into so many thoughts and drag you along. We have to be alert and attentive. Attention is inbuilt and ever-present. It is Consciousness, but for our understanding let us call it Attention. Even in sleep when you dream and wake up, something tells you that there was a dream and also tells you what kind of dream it was. That something is Attention. It is watchful of the dream even though your body and world did not exist while you were sleeping. It is present 24×7. Similarly, *so many people in the world sleep on a small cot. They toss and turn throughout the night, without their knowledge, yet they don't fall off the cot.* Something is making sure. That something is Attention. Another example is *that of a mother taking an afternoon nap near her baby who is sleeping in the cradle. A lot of noise will be around her. Husband watching a cricket match, children running around, and construction noise outside. With all that, she will be sleeping soundly. And yet, at the slightest sneeze or sound from the baby, she will instantly wake up.* There is a portion of Attention that is kept even in that deep sleep. Attention exists 24 hours.

Love and attention

In the human body, apart from the flesh and bones (physical body), you will find that there is this Attention (Gavanam or Consciousness). There is also Love (Anbu). When you are attentive, for example, *while reading a book or while locking the door as you leave the house, there need not be Love in that attention. While cooking you know when exactly to add salt, vs. when to add sugar. There is no Love in that attention.* So, it does not mean that whenever Attention is outward, Love should accompany it, but whenever Love comes from us, Attention will be there. *You hug someone with love. You are aware of who you are hugging. A girl out of true love will kiss her brother, sister, and her parents on the cheek or forehead, but when it is her husband, the kiss is on the lip.* See how well that attention is working. So whenever Love comes out, Attention follows but when Attention is coming out, Love need not come out. So, there are 2 portions. One is the physical: flesh & bones. The other has no name and form but is a mixture of Love and Attention.

How do we even know we have Love? Only because of Attention. Since Attention is ever-present. See, without Attention, Love would have been there, but we won't know what it would be like. Attention is always functioning. Even this is known to us because of Attention.

We are searching for Love

Even though there is unlimited Love in us, we are not showing or showering love 24 hours. It can come out but it doesn't. We don't create the situations to bring it out. We also don't have situations that favor it. *Vasanas*, likes, and dislikes interfere, make our attention focused on them and prevent our Love from coming out. If you make the effort and go beyond all this, then this unconditional unlimited Love will flow continuously as a *jiva nadhi*, a river of life filled with Attention and Love. This is what we are all actually yearning for. To reconnect with our own *jiva nadhi*. This yearning will never be quenched until you merge with this ever-flowing river inside you. Till then you will be looking for it outside. In relationships and things. For some time, the relationship will appear to give you that Love. But after some time, things start to sour, and when you sense that Love is not coming from that relationship you will start to yearn for it again. Like this you take on many, many births, yearning and searching for Love. It never ends. Because you are looking for borrowed love. Love from outside. That borrowed Love is not the same as the ever-flowing river inside you. It won't sustain.

Give. Don't Yearn

Instead, if you put in all your effort in bringing out the Love that is already inside you then one day or the other the yearning will totally end. So instead of YEARNING for Love outside, we need to change our mindset to GIVING Love. We have that channel, that *madai* (dam) of Love. Instead of opening our own dam, we are running here and there trying to open so many other *madais* like a *madayan!* (fool).

We continuously crave for Love. But the secret is that the more we give Love, the less the craving becomes. When we give Love, it feels good to us. Look at nature. *Look at the Sun. It gives light and heat continuously. Does it do it for itself? For the sun? No. It totally gives for others. And it does not mind whether you notice or not.* Mahaprabu asked us if we noticed the sun today, did we look at it, and thank it. How many people in the world notice the sun and thank it daily? Hardly any. But it does not stop giving. And you did not create the Sun. Your father or grandfather did not. It was created by the Creator before you arrived on this earth. All this has been created for you. Imagine how much Love that Creator has!

So the effort should be made in bringing out the love that is in us. And when we open up the spring of Love that is inside us, Attention will always accompany it. And the beautiful thing is that the first person to quench this thirst from this spring is us. We are first saturated and then others are. It is for this saturation that we are constantly looking for. We have had it, but we have lost it and have been searching ever since. *A dog that has been separated from its owner by several kilometers will continuously use its powerful smell ability to find the route to its owner and eventually reaches him. See how many wrong routes it would have tried and finally come to the right way. As it nears the destination, imagine how intensely, how fast it would have run.* This actually happened with a dog in the Rest house which came back after a separation of over 10 km. If this is possible for a dog, a more evolved being like a human definitely can reach his home.

We fell into this trap

At one point we were living as an ever-loving, ever-attentive being, flowing vibrantly. Somewhere we fell into this pothole, this trap, this dead body. Since then IT has been struggling, pulsating, *(thudippu)* pushing the boundaries of the body, and trying to come out of its death trap. The body is a hindrance, a torture to this spring of Love that had been flowing. That feeling of that ever-flowing love is the smell that the dog used to find its owner. The spring of Love keeps trying to find its home and not be limited to this body. That is why even someone who has had a loving nature for a long time can one day become frustrated and hateful *(veruppu)*, or simply bored, tired of it *(salippu)*. That Love he had in the beginning for someone or something has weakened. Now he is just hanging on just as a duty.

In all of us, that same *jiva nadhi* (river of life, love) is running. So, it keeps shaking us, as it is not its nature to be trapped in the body. You can now see why relationships are fragile. So many oaths are taken, *I will love you till death do us part.* But they don't last. That spring won't let you. Because it has become trapped in a small container called the body and is unable to flow freely as it did.

It is like taking a fish that is used to the deep, limitless ocean and putting it in a big pot or tank, which is then placed back in the ocean! Yes, it has water in the pot too but the freedom that it had in the ocean will constantly be missed by the fish. Something is missing. I don't know what it is. That 'something is missed' feeling will continuously disturb it. No matter what you do, clean the tank, show it all the love and feed it, that feeling of missing something will always be there with the fish. But if you take it to out of the tank, and set it free into the ocean, aha... imagine its joy. Because it no longer feels the suffering of the limitation it was constantly feeling. This is the plight of man. You might think, see how much I took care of that fish, it has no gratitude, etc. This is what is happening daily with us. Husband disappointed by wife, wife by husband, etc. The fish escaped to the ocean. But since you are bound by the world, there is no escape. So you keep complaining, keep yearning.

In all of us there is the 'ocean-fish'. It is living in a limited pot. It is suffering, yearning for the ocean. If it finds its way out of the pot and into the ocean, its joy is unbound. *The fish that lives in the ocean and shows the fish trapped in the tank the way to come out of the tank and swim into the ocean, is the Guru.*

What to do?

If you look at the example of the fish closely, you will see that in reality the fish has not been moved to a small tank on dry land. It is still in the ocean. But someone, something has given it the wrong idea that it is limited to a small circle, a small area in the ocean. This idea has been implanted so strongly, that it cannot ever imagine that it has the whole ocean for itself. It suffers endlessly, thinking it is so limited to this dirty small patch. So, what separates the fish from the vast ocean? Just one thought. Imagine how powerful that thought must be. Therefore, tremendous work must be done in order to get rid of it.

Everything must be dropped, given second priority to this task. First we need to withdraw attention from the body. I am not the body, so its needs, its sufferings, and its joys are in no way connected to me. Keep on bringing back the Attention inward. Don't squander it on the body. This itself is so hard. Then you need to disassociate from the World. So many traps are there and they are continuous. You have to disconnect as much as possible. Limit the connection only to the most essential. Keep on bringing back the attention inward. Don't squander it on the world. It will drag you away. Whenever the Attention begins to drift, be alert and bring it back inward. Otherwise, it will multiply so fast that you won't know when you've been dragged out totally.

Be like the crane that is looking for the big fish. It waits on the banks of the river patiently, with tremendous attention. Not even a single movement. Even if many small fish go by it, the crane waits. A big fish may come near, but it will wait until that fish is within its reach. It will not be distracted by anything. Even though one doesn't realize he is Atma, he is Atma. This will be learned when you are totally still. Our distractions come from the world, and from within us. *It is like trying to keep the surface of the water still to see the reflection of the moon, but you are continuously throwing rocks from the outside. Will it ever be still?* When you stop and the water starts to settle down, so many frogs (your thoughts, memories, imaginations) from inside the pond are trying to jump out. The water is never still. Don't keep throwing stones in or letting the frogs jump out if you want the water to be still.

Being in Surrender is the best way. Surrender to whom? To a living Jnani. When you surrender to God or a dead Jnani it is highly possible that your mind is cheating you. It is entirely a one-way communication. Your mind will create a comfort zone. You go to the ashram or temple regularly; do a few routines and believe you are in Surrender. The surrender and its boundaries are set by you! A dead master will not demand anything. But with a real living Master, he will demand the surrender. He knows whether you are in surrender or not and will keep pointing out whenever you are not, whenever you are being cheated by your mind. And since a real Master is Love and Attention personified, just being in his presence will have its effect on you over time. You will slow down naturally. He knows where the blocks are in you and creates situations for them to be destroyed. Then his love flows into you. His flow makes the flow happen in you. It will happen. All you have to do is to be in complete Surrender. Nothing else.

Devotion, Bhakti can help tremendously here. Keep on thanking the creator. Before you sit for Meditation immerse yourself in *Irai Bhakti* or *Guru Bhakti* (devotion to God, Guru). Let that be the foundation. Then it will turn into *Dhyanam*, Meditation.

Bhakti then Jnana

Sri Mahaprabu clearly points out the risks inherent in starting with the approach of Jnana. He then shows a time-tested and much easier path where you begin with Devotion, Surrender and Love. And most importantly he gives us a proper understanding of what the steps are to get there.

Knowledge vs. Love

More than *Arivu Parivarthanai* (sharing of knowledge), *Anbu Parivarthanai* (sharing of Love) is important. In knowledge sharing, something might be forgotten, not understood, etc. but in the flow of love, there is no question of forgetting, etc. It is beyond the mind. It is from the heart. If a person cannot change someone by imparting knowledge they can definitely change them through love. *A child may not be effective, but if the mother is continuously loving, there is a high chance for him to go beyond his ineffectiveness. But if she is not loving and criticizes his ineffectiveness regularly, there is a high chance that he will not improve. In fact, even if he is highly effective if the love from the mother isn't there, she has failed because he might have knowledge but that lack of love will affect him.* This world needs change through love. If you neglect someone from a love standpoint but focus on knowledge, you are the fool. But if you fail in giving knowledge but give a lot of love, you are the smart one, the successful one. Because what is needed is only love. Love is the energy that flows. The stuff on which enlightenment stands is Love.

Mahaprabu asked a disciple, just as a measurement: The amount of love you have for God, for Bhagavan, do you have that much love for the person next to you? Tell me honestly. Yes or No.

Disciple: No.

Mahaprabu: Where is God? In all! That doesn't mean you take a cobra and put it on your lap. That's why even when you kill a cobra that poses a danger, you pray and kill it. The prayer should be: God is the one who is in both of us. This killing of you is done with love, so that you may change your form and ascend to the next birth. So don't take this as *suffering*. It is an *offering!!*

So, we should continuously move towards becoming loving, by creating situations to express love. If you want to move towards God, you cannot do that without love blossoming in you. That is the proof that you are moving towards God. If you say that you want to move toward God but won't be loving toward others, then you have a psychological disorder. You i.e. your ego has created a God and takes pride in loving it. What a psycho. So many people, so-called staunch devotees are in this mode. All they have done is satisfy their ego. They pick a God or a world-famous Guru and take pride in it. But when you come to a real Master, he will see the symptoms in you right away. He will know that what you have is not natural. He won't bother about what all the symptoms are. He knows that it is not natural. That's enough. He will create situations to tackle that. *For example, if someone comes for a Covid test, they will simply tell you whether it is positive or negative for Covid. He won't diagnose what other issues you have etc.*

The real practice

So, to the extent to which you love God, you must develop that same love toward others. Even if they aren't good by your standards, you need to remember that what is there also, is the same *Paramatma*. You don't even need to express that love. Just have to fill yourself with it. That is Surrender. Only if you are in Surrender, saying "O Lord, I know it is you there (in that person). Go ahead, scold me, shout at me, hurt me, I am not going to do anything to react and hurt you." That ability to stay silent, without reacting, by thinking of God at that moment when the reaction is about to spring, strengthens you tremendously. That is the real practice. To remember God in that situation is hard. Even though you have some concept or form of God or Guru, it is hard. If that is hard, imagine... Can you remember 'All is Brahman' or 'Who Am I'? It is much harder.

But what is everyone trying to practice? Pure *Advaita Jnana*. The hardest thing to do. Instead of doing that which is much easier. Remembering that God/Guru is in all forms, and staying calm even though the other person is yelling at me, is relatively easier. When you don't react, what happens? The *brahmananda sakthi*, Supreme Power that is in you connects with the same *brahmananda sakthi* that is the Guru/God. Because of that connection the response that comes from you will be the perfect one for that situation. So, the most important thing is to not react in situations. But you cannot make 'I won't react, I will be calm' as a practice. It might work for a short while but it won't last long. That is why you bring God, Surrender. Without God and Surrender, you yourself are in control. Since you are in control, you will decide what the threshold is, and what the tolerance is. How long can you be tolerant? Since you are doing the practice with your ego, it (the ego) will decide when to break its tolerance. At that point, it will erupt saying 'I have been patient for so long. I've had it. I cannot take this any longer.' All the pent-up control will now blow up. And you will justify your actions further. But if you leave it in the hands of God, saying 'O God, only you can give me the strength, please let me not react', you have given the control to whom? To God. So you won't break it easily. And if you do that and still react, you will not justify your reaction. Instead, you will feel bad. Therefore you will ask forgiveness and pray for more strength and move on.

Bhakti vs. Jnana

Sri Buddha focused on pure Jnana. So many people focus on pure Jnana. That approach requires that you begin with Arivu, knowledge, your mind. But to approach God, whose nature is Love, will you start with knowledge or Love? The approach of Jnana is highly risky. It may be beautiful but is very mind-oriented. You will keep on satisfying your mind, collecting more and more information. Even though love could have blossomed from the beginning, it does not because you have started with knowledge and mind. The success rate is low and even if one is really strong it will still take a lot of time. With *Bhakti marga* (path of devotion) you start with love. From the beginning, love starts blossoming. So it has a high chance of success. Because of the step-by-step growth of love in you, the impurities in you start to disappear, good qualities rise, then you go to Nirguna, attain Brahman, and with it comes all Knowledge. But in the Jnana path, if you ever get there, Love will finally come. But there is no assurance that you will reach there in the first place. It may come after several janmas (births). But in Bhakti, it starts with Love and will eventually end in Wisdom. You can be assured.

Paramahamsa mixed Bhakti and Jnana. He wants you to eat the jackfruit, and to make it easy, he peels it, dips it in honey, and shows you the dripping honey. That is Bhakti. It can pull anyone. Following pure Jnana is very difficult. Because all around you, people are not following Jnana (referring to most humans). *For example, say there is a traffic signal that is mostly red. Yet you wait each time for it to turn green. But everyone around you is going through the red light (there is never any police there). One day or the other, chances are high that you will also lose your values and go through the red light.* But with Bhakti it is the opposite. So many around you are following it. That is how Nature has made it.

When it comes to knowledge vs. feeling, the latter always wins. You might have all the knowledge stored in you, but when a stressful or new situation comes, it is your feelings that take over. You will automatically look to the higher power. *Even a great batsman like Sachin, let's say in two matches he gets bowled out in the first ball, the 3rd time you think he will be comfortable and rely on only his skill? He will pray. Look at the Covid situation. People are now living locked up, in fear. Since they are helpless, they are naturally looking toward God.*

Love and Devotion is the way

So increase your faith genuinely. Not as a technique for you to stay calm. There must be genuine love. Strengthen your Surrender. "O, God. In all situations, You must come to my mind." Will this attitude increase or reduce your Ego? It will reduce it. Anything to reduce Ego alone will take you towards Jnana. So what is the benchmark of progress? In any situation, how loving I have been. We can feel it. Nature has given us that ability. You can feel it both ways. If you have been loving or not loving. If you are unable to feel it, the Guru is the mirror for you to know. He will point out what is love, what is not love and even what is weakness. At one point you will know. Till then what is needed is Satsang. To know what is permanent/impermanent, Love/Not Love, Strength/Weakness, to gain that discriminative ability is why you need Satsang. The Guru makes you know through various situations. So make this your scale. 'Am I filled with love or not filled with love'. In everyone, that Godliness is there. You should feel that equally in all beings. You don't need to express love equally to all, but you should feel that love equally. Then you are flowering and becoming a ripe fruit. This is real growth. If you don't, then the growth is stinted. Disease sets in. You rot like a tree affected by disease.

Since we are blessed with intelligence we should inspect and see where we are stuck, fix it, and move forward. Keep the urge that you should be filled with love for everyone, whether you express it or not. That is why it is said "*Unnal nanmai adaya vo, theemai adyavo adhiya patta anaithu uyirgalukkum nee kattura anbu*" The love you show towards beings to whom you are going to do good, and towards those beings to whom you are going to do harm!. When you are nice to someone you will be able to show love more easily. That's not surprising. But if you are going to hurt someone, will you show love? It is difficult but it is possible. You should. Like the example of the snake, I gave you. Once you decide to kill it, you have to hurt it. But you can do it with love as discussed earlier. So the *manobhavam* (mental attitude) is what is important, not the action! We have to bring that *manobhavam* into our actions. But we cannot remember to do it for each situation accordingly. Instead, if you live with the attitude at all times, that all is God, that will take care of it. Only that will work. Never believe your mind is capable of remembering.

How to be loving – The steps

We are good. We are always good. We are Atma, limitless, deathless. Only our actions might be bad. Everyone commits mistakes. It is due to ignorance. That we can correct. And while correcting we should be aware that we should not commit the same mistake. Unknowingly we may commit a new mistake, but knowingly we should not commit the same mistake. That we should try. Not cry! It is for correcting that, an opportunity is given. That is called human birth. I (Mahaprabu) have made so many mistakes. Countless mistakes. I made them from countless to less count!

That is why Mahaprabu is emphasizing Love first. That's why all this talk. And this Love I am talking about is not the love that a person has for another person. That love is based on identity, so behind it is *ahankaram*, ego. I am talking about the Love that you place for God. First, believe in that Supreme Power who has created all this and maintains all this. I am calling that God. Secondly, Love that immensely. Thirdly, feel that Love continuously. Fourth: Once you do that, you should start feeling that same Love towards all beings, living and non-living, since it is that Supreme Power that created them all. You don't need to express it to all, but you don't suppress it either! So first check, do you have Love for the God that I am talking about? If not, start there. Only then can you shower 'that same Love' on all beings.

When you start loving that Supreme Power, knowing that He is doing everything and He will always do it right, your surrender will become strong. Then because of the Love you have for Him, you will feel that Love inside you. Since it is coming from within. Once that happens, then that Love will transfer to all his creations. It happens Not directly from you to them but through Him.

By doing all this, we know for a fact that our lives will become better. We know this for a fact. We just have to implement it. This is the path. It is simple. Just follow it.

What more do you need to know about Atma Jnanam? What more do you have to read? Nothing. Just hold on to this and keep moving up. I am doing it moment to moment. You also join me. The Master is not doing this because of some duty. Because of his Love, he is sharing it with you. It is his responsibility, not his duty. Heart has Love. Love has Responsibility. Mind has knowledge. Knowledge makes it a duty. As we are loving God, it is the Master's responsibility to show the path. It is not his duty. The Guru is the initiator, facilitator, and co-traveler but it is your journey.

Satsang with Sri Mahaprabu

May the grace of Bhagavan Ramana Maharshi, Sri Annamalai Swami, Sri Mahaprabu and all the Brahma Jnanis guide you and protect you.

Sri Mahaprabu conducts Satsang regularly in Paliapattu (8 Km from Ramanashramam) during the weekends. Seekers who are very eager to lose their ego and rediscover their true nature are requested to contact us by sending an email to annamalaiswamytrust@gmail.com.

Please make sure to include your name, contact information, nationality, your present life situation and a detailed background about yourself.

Thank you

Sri Satguru Annamalai Swamigal Spiritual Trust

Publications

By Sri Satguru Annamalai Swamigal Spiritual Trust

In Tamil

Sri Bhagavanum Adiyenum
Kadaisi Varthaigal

In Telugu

Bhagavan Adugujadalalo
Annamalai Swami Anthima Sambashanamulu

In English

Nectar Drops: The Diary of Sri Annamalai Swamigal
Nectar Drops: The Diary of Sri Annamalai Swamigal, Digital Edition
Living by the words of Bhagavan
Living by the words of Bhagavan, Digital Edition
Annamalai Swami – Final Talks
Annamalai Swami – Final Talks, Digital Edition
Return To The Source – Volume 1

CDs and DVDs

Ribhu Gita chanting in Tamil by Sri Annamalai Swami
Video interview of Sri Annamalai Swami - Jim Lemkin
Video interview of Sri Annamalai Swami - Madhukar Thompson
Video talk of Sri Annamalai Swami - Meera
Video interview of Sri Annamalai Swami - Arunachala Ashrama

Websites

A website dedicated to Sri Annamalai Swamigal is available at
www.SriAnnamalaiSwami.org. A website dedicated to Sri Mahaprabu is
available at www.SriMahaprabu.org.

Printed in Great Britain
by Amazon

40109516R00086